COLLECTED WORKS OF RENÉ GUÉNON

THE SYMBOLISM OF THE CROSS

RENÉ GUÉNON

THE SYMBOLISM
OF THE CROSS

Translator
Angus Macnab

SOPHIA PERENNIS

HILLSDALE NY

Originally published in French as
Le Symbolisme de la Croix
© Les Éditions de la Maisnie 1931
Fourth, revised edition 2001
Second Impression 2004
Third edition, Sophia Perennis, Ghent 1996
First and Second editions, 1962, 1975,
Luzac & Company, London
English translation © Sophia Perennis 2001

Series editor: James R. Wetmore

For information, address:
Sophia Perennis, P.O. Box 611
Hillsdale NY 12529
sophiaperennis.com

Library of Congress Cataloging-in-Publication Data

Guénon, René
[Symbolisme de la croix. English]
The symbolism of the Cross / René Guénon ; translated by
Angus Macnab ; 4th rev. ed.

p. cm. — (Collected works of René Guénon)
Includes index.
ISBN 0 900588 65 9 (pbk: alk. paper)
ISBN 0 900588 66 7 (cloth: alk. paper)
1. Crosses 2. Symbolism. I. Macnab, Angus II. Title.
BL604.C7G813 2001
291.3'7—dc21   2001001096

To the venerated memory of
al-Shaykh ʿAbd al-Raḥmān ʿIlaysh al-Kabīr
al-ʿĀlim al-Mālikī al-Maghribī,
to whom I owe the first
idea of this book

Mesr al-Qāhirah, 1329–1349 H

CONTENTS

EDITORIAL NOTE

THE PAST CENTURY HAS WITNESSED an erosion of earlier cultural values as well as a blurring of the distinctive characteristics of the world's traditional civilizations, giving rise to philosophic and moral relativism, multiculturalism, and dangerous fundamentalist reactions. As early as the 1920s, the French metaphysician René Guénon (1886–1951) had diagnosed these tendencies and presented what he believed to be the only possible reconciliation of the legitimate, although apparently conflicting, demands of outward religious forms, 'exoterisms', with their essential core, 'esoterism'. His works are characterized by a foundational critique of the modern world coupled with a call for intellectual reform; a renewed examination of metaphysics, the traditional sciences, and symbolism, with special reference to the ultimate unanimity of all spiritual traditions; and finally, a call to the work of spiritual realization. Despite their wide influence, translation of Guénon's works into English has so far been piecemeal. The *Sophia Perennis* edition is intended to fill the urgent need to present them in a more authoritative and systematic form. A complete list of Guénon's works, given in the order of their original publication in French, follows this note.

The Symbolism of the Cross, together with its companion volume *The Multiple States of the Being* and the earlier and more specialized *Man and His Becoming according to the Vedānta*, constitute the core of Guénon's writing on the doctrines of tradional metaphysics. Guénon applies these doctrines in his critique of modernity in such works as *The Crisis of the Modern World* and *The Reign of Quantity and the Signs of the Times*, and invokes them to help explain the nature of initiation and of initiatic organizations in such works as *Perspectives on Initiation* and *Initiation and Spiritual Realization*.

The Symbolism of the Cross is a major doctrinal study of the central symbol of Christianity from the standpoint of the universal metaphysical tradition, the 'perennial philosophy' as it is called in the West. As Guénon points out, the cross is one of the most universal of all symbols and is far from belonging to Christianity alone. Indeed, Christians have sometimes tended to lose sight of its symbolical significance and to regard it as no more than the sign of a historical event. By restoring to the cross its full spiritual value as a symbol, but without in any way detracting from its historical importance for Christianity, Guénon has performed a task of inestimable importance which perhaps only he, with his unrivalled knowledge of the symbolic languages of both East and West, was qualified to perform.

Guénon often uses words or expressions set off in 'scare quotes'. To avoid clutter, single quotation marks have been used throughout. As for transliterations, Guénon was more concerned with phonetic fidelity than academic usage. The system adopted here reflects the views of scholars familiar both with the languages and Guénon's writings. Brackets indicate editorial insertions, or, within citations, Guénon's additions. Wherever possible, references have been updated, and English editions substituted.

The translation is based on the work of Angus Macnab, reviewed for accuracy and revised by James Wetmore. For help with selected chapters and proofreading thanks go to Brian and Michelle Latham, John Champoux, Allan Dewar, and John Ahmed Herlihy. A special debt of thanks is owed to Cecil Bethell, who revised and proofread the text at several stages and provided the index. Cover design by Michael Buchino and Gray Henry, based on a drawing of band design details from Grecian pottery of the sixth century BC, by Guénon's friend and collaborator Ananda K. Coomaraswamy.

THE WORKS
OF RENÉ GUÉNON

PREFACE

AS EXPLAINED at the beginning of *Man and His Becoming according to the Vedānta*, that work was intended to form the first of a series of studies that, as occasion might demand, would either give a direct account of certain aspects of the Eastern metaphysical doctrines, or else adapt them in such a way as might seem most intelligible and profitable, while always remaining strictly faithful to their spirit. That series of studies had to be shelved for a time, because circumstances called for other works dealing with various contingent applications of these doctrines; but even here, care was taken never to lose sight of those metaphysical principles on which all true traditional teaching solely rests.

In *Man and His Becoming* it was shown how a being such as man is envisaged by a traditional doctrine of a purely metaphysical order. The exposition was confined as closely as possible to the doctrine itself, and any departure was aimed merely at bringing out concordances between that doctrine and other traditional forms. Our works have never purported to remain exclusively within one given traditional form; indeed, the acceptance of such a restriction would be extremely difficult in view of the essential unity of tradition underlying the diversity of more or less outward forms, which are really no more than different garments clothing one and the same truth. In general, we have taken the point of view of the Hindu doctrines as our central one, for reasons that have been explained elsewhere;[1] but that can be no reason for failing to make use, whenever it seems advisable, of modes of expression drawn from other traditions—always provided, of course, that they are authentic ones, that is, traditions that can be called regular or orthodox, taking

1. *East and West*, pt. 2, chap. 4.

2 THE SYMBOLISM OF THE CROSS

those terms in the sense we have explained elsewhere.[2] In the present book, that will be done even oftener than before, because this time there is no question of keeping to a certain branch of doctrine as found in one given civilization. The purpose of the work is to explain a symbol that is common to almost all traditions, a fact that would seem to indicate its direct attachment to the great primordial tradition.

In this connection it is necessary to stress from the outset one point of particular importance, in order to dispel certain confusions that are unhappily all too frequent today, namely the fundamental difference between 'synthesis' and 'syncretism'. Syncretism consists in assembling from the outside a number of more or less incongruous elements, which, when so regarded, can never be truly unified; in short, it is a kind of eclecticism, with all the fragmentariness and incoherence that this always implies. Syncretism, then, is something purely outward and superficial; the elements taken from every quarter and put together in this way can never amount to anything more than borrowings that are incapable of being effectively integrated into a doctrine worthy of the name.

Synthesis on the other hand is carried out essentially from within, by which we mean that it properly consists in envisaging things in the unity of their principle, in seeing how they are derived from and dependent on that principle, and thus uniting them—or rather becoming aware of their real unity—by virtue of a wholly inward bond, inherent in what is most profound in their nature.

To apply the above criteria to the present context, syncretism can be recognized wherever one finds elements borrowed from different traditional forms and assembled together without any awareness that there is only one single doctrine, of which these forms are so many different expressions or so many adaptations to particular conditions related to given circumstances of time and place. In such a case nothing valid can emerge from the collection. To use a readily comprehensible comparison, we shall get not an organized whole

2. *Introduction to the Study of the Hindu Doctrines*, pt. 3, chap. 3; *Man and His Becoming according to the Vedānta* (hereafter cited as *Man and His Becoming*), chap. 1.

but a formless pile of debris, which is useless because it lacks anything that could give it a unity like that of a living being or a harmonious building. Indeed, the characteristic feature of syncretism, by the very fact of its outwardness, is its inability to achieve such a unity. Synthesis, on the contrary, will exist when one starts from unity itself and never loses sight of it throughout the multiplicity of its manifestations; this moreover implies an ability to see beyond forms and an awareness of the principial truth, which clothes itself in forms in order to express and communicate itself in the measure in which this is possible. Given such awareness, one is at liberty to make use of one or another of those forms, just as one may use different languages to translate the same thought for the benefit of different people—something that certain traditions symbolically denote as the 'gift of tongues'.

The concordances between all traditional forms may be said to represent genuine 'synonymies'; that is how we regard them, and just as the explanation of certain things may be easier in one language than in another, so one of these forms may be better fitted than others for expounding certain truths and rendering them easier to understand. Hence in each case it is perfectly legitimate to make use of the form that seems most suitable for the purpose in hand; there is no objection to passing from one form to another, provided one is really aware of their equivalence, which can only be the case if one views them in the light of their common principle. In this way, no syncretism will arise; indeed the latter can only be a product of a 'profane' outlook, which is incompatible with the very idea of the 'sacred science' to which these studies exclusively refer.

The cross is a symbol that in its various forms is met with almost everywhere, and from the most remote times; it is therefore far from belonging peculiarly and exclusively to the Christian tradition, as some might be tempted to believe. It must even be stated that Christianity, at any rate in its outward and generally known aspect, seems to have somewhat lost sight of the symbolic character of the cross and come to regard it as no longer anything but the sign of an historical event. Actually, these two points of view are in no way mutually exclusive; indeed the second is in a sense a consequence of the first, but this way of looking at things is so strange to the great majority of people today that it deserves dwelling on for a moment in order to avoid possible misunderstandings.

The fact is that people too often tend to think that if a symbolical meaning is admitted, the literal or historical sense must be rejected; such a view can only result from unawareness of the law of correspondence that is the very foundation of all symbolism. By virtue of this law, each thing, proceeding as it does from a metaphysical principle from which it derives all its reality, translates or expresses that principle in its own fashion and in accordance with its own order of existence, so that from one order to another all things are linked together and correspond in such a way as to contribute to the universal and total harmony, which, in the multiplicity of manifestation, can be likened to a reflection of the principial unity itself.

For this reason the laws of a lower domain can always be taken to symbolize realities of a higher order, wherein resides their own profoundest cause, which is at once their principle and their end; we would recall in this connection the error of the modern 'naturalistic' interpretations of ancient traditional doctrines, interpretations that purely and simply reverse the hierarchy of relationships between the different orders of reality. Thus, the purpose of symbols and myths has never been—as has often been wrongly alleged—to represent the movement of the heavenly bodies, the truth being that while they often do contain figures inspired by that movement they are intended to express, analogically, something very different, because the laws of that movement are a physical translation of the metaphysical principles on which they depend. What is true of astronomical phenomena can equally and for the same reason be applied to all other kinds of natural phenomena: these phenomena, by the very fact that they are derived from higher and transcendent principles, truly serve to symbolize those principles. Obviously, this in no way affects the reality possessed by the phenomena as such in the order of existence they belong to; on the contrary, it is the very basis of that reality, for apart from their dependence on their principles, all things would be mere non-entity.

This holds good for historical facts no less than for anything else: they likewise conform to the law of correspondence just mentioned, and thereby, in their own mode, translate higher realities, of which they are so to speak a human expression. We would add that from our point of view (which obviously is quite different from that of the profane historians),[3] it is this that gives to these facts the greater part of their significance. This symbolical character, while common to all historical events, is bound to be particularly clear-cut in the case of events connected with what may be called 'sacred history'; thus it is recognizable in a most striking way in all the circumstances of the life of Christ. If the foregoing has been properly grasped, it will at once be apparent not only that there is no reason for denying the reality of these events and treating them as mere myths, but on the contrary that these events had to be such as they were, and could not have been otherwise; it is clearly impossible to attribute a sacred character to something devoid of all transcendent significance. In particular, if Christ died on the cross, it can be said that this was by reason of the symbolic value that the cross possesses in itself and that has always been recognized by all traditions; thus, without diminishing in any way its historical significance, the latter may be regarded as directly derived from the symbolical significance that goes with it.

A further consequence of this law of correspondence is the plurality of meanings contained in every symbol. Anything and everything can in fact be regarded as representing not only the metaphysical principles, but also realities of all orders higher than its own, even if still contingent, for these realities, on which it also more or less directly depends, play the part of 'secondary causes' in respect of it; likewise, the effect can always be taken as a symbol of the cause, at any level whatsoever, because it is nothing more than the expression of something inherent in the nature of that cause. These multiple and hierarchically superimposed symbolical meanings are not in any way mutually exclusive. On the contrary, they are perfectly concordant because they express the applications of one and the same principle to different orders; thus they complete and corroborate one another, while being integrated in the harmony of

---

3. 'Historical truth itself is stable only when it is derived from the Principle' (*Chuang Tzu*, chap. 25).

the total synthesis. This moreover is what makes symbolism a far less narrowly limited language than ordinary speech, and renders it best fitted to express and convey certain truths. The possibilities of conception it opens up are truly limitless, and it is for this reason that it constitutes the initiatic language par excellence, the indispensable vehicle of all traditional teaching.

Thus the cross, like any other symbol, can be regarded according to manifold senses; however, it is not our intention to develop them all equally here, and there are some that will merely be touched on along the way. The essential object before us is the metaphysical sense, the first and most important of all since it is properly the principial one, all other applications being more or less secondary and contingent. If we do consider some of these, it will always be with the ultimate object of attaching them to the metaphysical order, for this is obviously what gives them their value and legitimacy, in conformity with the conception—quite forgotten by the modern world—of 'traditional science'.

1

MULTIPLICITY OF
STATES OF THE BEING

ANY BEING, whether human or otherwise, can clearly be envisaged from a large number—it can even be said, an indefinite number—of points of view; these are very unequal in importance, but are all equally legitimate in their respective domains, provided that none of them seeks to encroach beyond its own proper limits, or, what is still worse, to become exclusive and end by denying the others. Granted that this is so, and that accordingly none of these points of view, not even the most secondary and contingent of them, can be denied the place belonging to it by the mere fact that it answers to some possibility, it is no less obvious on the other hand that from the metaphysical point of view, which alone concerns us here, the consideration of a being in its individual aspect is necessarily insufficient, since 'metaphysical' is synonymous with 'universal'. Hence no doctrine that confines itself to the consideration of individual beings can merit the name of metaphysics, whatever may be its interest and value in other respects; such a doctrine can always be called 'physical' in the original sense of the word, because it lies exclusively within the realm of 'nature'—that is, of manifestation—with the further restriction that it envisages only formal manifestation, and even more especially one of the states that constitute the latter.

Far from being an absolute and complete unity in himself, as most Western philosophers—at any rate all modern ones—would regard him, the individual in reality constitutes but a relative and fragmentary unity. He is not a closed and self-sufficient whole, an 'enclosed system' after the fashion of Leibnitz's 'monad'; and the notion of 'individual substance', thus understood, to which these philosophers generally attach so much importance, has no truly metaphysical bearing: fundamentally, it is nothing else but the notion of the 'subject' in logic, and while it may undoubtedly possess great usefulness in that respect, it cannot be legitimately carried beyond the limits of that special point of view. The individual, even when considered in the full extension of which he is capable, is not a total being, but only a particular state of manifestation of a being, a state subject to certain special and determined conditions of existence and occupying a certain place in the indefinite series of the states of the total being. What characterizes a state as individual is the presence of form among these conditions of existence; it is obvious however that this form need not necessarily be conceived as spatial, for it is so only in the corporeal world, space being precisely one of the conditions that properly define that world.[1]

Reference must be made here, at least in summary fashion, to the fundamental distinction between the 'Self' and the 'ego', or between the 'personality' and the 'individuality', which has been dealt with more fully elsewhere.[2] The 'Self', as has been pointed out, is the transcendent and permanent principle of which the manifested being, the human being for example, is no more than a transient and contingent modification, which moreover can in no wise affect this principle. Immutable in its own nature, the Self develops its possibilities in all the modalities of realization, indefinite in their multitude, which for the total being amount to so many states, each of which has its limiting and determining conditions of existence, and only one of which constitutes the portion—or rather particular determination—of this being that is the 'ego' or human individuality. Again, this development is only such, in reality, when viewed from the standpoint of manifestation, outside of which everything must necessarily be in perfect simultaneity in the 'eternal present'; on that account the 'permanent actuality' of the Self is not affected thereby. The Self is thus the principle by which all the states of the being exist, each in its own proper sphere, which may be called a degree of existence; and this must be understood not only of the manifested states—whether individual, like the human state, or

1. See *Man and His Becoming*, chaps. 2 and 10.
2. Ibid., chap. 2.

supra-individual, in other words whether formal or formless—but also, though the word 'exist' then becomes inadequate, of the non-manifested states, comprising all those possibilities that, by their very nature, do not admit of any manifestation, as well as the possibilities of manifestation themselves in their principial state; but this Self subsists by itself alone, for in the total and indivisible unity of its innermost nature it has not, and cannot have, any principle external to itself.

It has just been said that the word 'exist' cannot properly be applied to the non-manifested, or in other words to the principial state; in fact, taken in its strictly etymological sense (from the Latin *ex-stare*), this word indicates the being that is dependent on a principle other than itself, or, in other words, one that is not for itself its own sufficient cause—in short, a contingent being, which is the same thing as a manifested being.[3] When we speak of Existence, we thus mean universal manifestation, with all the states or degrees that it contains, each of which may equally be described as a 'world', one of a series that is indefinite in its multiplicity; but this term no longer fits the degree of pure Being, the principle of all manifestation though itself non-manifested, nor *a fortiori* does it fit that which lies beyond Being itself.

Before all else, it must be stated that Existence, regarded universally according to the above definition, is unique in its inner nature, just as Being is one in itself; indeed this unity of Existence derives directly from the unity of Being, since universal Existence is nothing but the integral manifestation of Being, or, to be more exact, the realization in manifested mode, of all the possibilities that Being implies and contains principially in its very unity. Again, like the unity of Being on which it is founded, the 'unicity' of Existence (if we may employ this term, which may seem a neologism)[4] does not exclude the multiplicity of the modes of manifestation or become

3. Hence, strictly speaking, the common expression 'the existence of God' is meaningless, whether by 'God' one means Being, as is generally intended, or, *a fortiori*, the Supreme Principle which is beyond Being.

4. This term permits us to render more exactly the equivalent Arabic expression *Waḥdat al-wujūd*. On the distinction to be drawn between the 'unicity' of Existence, the 'unity' of Being, and the 'non-duality' of the Supreme Principle, see *Man and His Becoming*, chap. 6.

affected thereby, since it equally comprehends all these modes by the very fact that they are equally possible, this possibility implying that each of them shall be realized under the conditions appropriate to it. Hence, in its 'unicity', Existence implies, as has just been explained, an indefinitude of degrees, corresponding to all the modes of universal manifestation; and this indefinite multiplicity of the degrees of Existence implies correlatively, for any being considered in its totality, an equally indefinite multiplicity of possible states, each of which must be realized in a given degree of Existence.

This multiplicity of the states of the being, which is a fundamental metaphysical truth, holds good even when one confines oneself to considering the states of manifestation, as has just been done here, and as must always be done whenever Existence alone is under discussion; hence it holds good *a fortiori* if one considers the states of both manifestation and non-manifestation at once, the combination of which constitutes Being in its totality; the latter is then no longer envisaged in the sole domain of Existence, even taken in the whole integrality of its extension, but in the unlimited realm of universal possibility. It should be clearly understood in fact that Existence comprises only possibilities of manifestation, and even then with the restriction that these possibilities be conceived only insofar as they actually manifest themselves, for insofar as they are not manifested—that is, principially—they are at the degree of Being. Existence then is far from covering the whole of possibility, conceived as truly universal and total, that is to say outside and beyond all limitations—including even that first limitation constituting the most primordial determination of all, namely the affirmation of pure Being.[5]

When the states of non-manifestation of a being are in question, there is again a distinction to be drawn between the degree of Being and what lies beyond; in the latter case, it is clear that the term

---

5. It should be noted that in order to construct their systems philosophers always seek, consciously or unconsciously, to set some limit on universal Possibility; this is contradictory, but it is demanded by the very nature of a system as such. It might be quite interesting to write a history of the different modern philosophical theories, which are the ones that most commonly show this systematic character, from the standpoint of the limitations attributed to universal Possibility.

'Being' itself can no longer be strictly applied in its proper sense; yet limitations of language oblige us to retain it for want of a better, while not attributing to it any but a purely analogical and symbolical value; it would otherwise be impossible to speak at all of what one is dealing with. We may accordingly continue to speak of the total being as at the same time both manifested in certain of its states and non-manifested in others, without thereby in any way implying that in the latter case it is necessary to stop short at the consideration of what corresponds to the degree which is properly that of Being.[6]

The states of non-manifestation are essentially extra-individual, and, like the principial 'Self' from which they cannot be separated, they cannot in any way be individualized; as for the states of manifestation, some are individual while others are non-individual, a difference corresponding as has been explained to the distinction between formal and formless manifestation. If we consider the case of man in particular, his present individuality, which constitutes the human state properly speaking, is only one state of manifestation among an indefinitude of others, which must all be conceived as equally possible and thereby as existing, at least virtually if not effectively realized by the being whom we are considering, under a relative and partial aspect, in this individual human state.

---

6. On the state that corresponds to the degree of Being, and the unconditioned state that lies beyond, see *Man and His Becoming*, chaps. 15 and 16.

2

UNIVERSAL MAN

THE EFFECTIVE REALIZATION of the being's multiple states is related to the conception that various traditional doctrines, including Islamic esoterism, denote by the term 'Universal Man',[1] a conception that, as has been said elsewhere, establishes a constitutive analogy between universal manifestation and its individual human modality, or, to use the language of Western Hermeticism, between the 'macrocosm' and the 'microcosm'.[2] This idea may moreover be envisaged at different levels and with various extensions, the same analogy remaining valid in all these cases;[3] thus, it may be restricted to humanity itself, considered either in its specific nature or even in its social organization, for on this analogy the institution of the castes, among other applications, essentially rests.[4] At another and more extended level, the same notion may embrace the domain of existence corresponding to the whole of a given state of the being,

---

1. 'Universal Man' (in Arabic *al-Insān al-kāmil*) is at the same time 'Primordial Man' (*al-Insān al-qadīm*); it is the *Adam Qadmon* of the Hebrew Kabbalah; it is also the 'King' (*Wang*) of the Far-Eastern tradition (*Tao Te Ching*, chap. 25). In Islamic esoterism there exist a large number of treatises by different authors on *al-Insān al-kāmil*; the only ones that will be mentioned here, as being particularly important from the present point of view, are those of Muḥyi 'd-Dīn ibn al-Arabī and 'Abd al-Karīm al-Jīlī.

2. The use we make of these terms, as also of certain others, has already been explained elsewhere, and there does not seem to be any need to be overly concerned at the abuse sometimes made of them (*Man and His Becoming*, chap. 6). These terms, of Greek origin, also have their exact Arabic equivalents (*al-kawn al-kabīr* and *al-kawn as-saghīr*), which are taken in the same sense.

3. A similar observation might be made about the theory of cycles, which is ultimately only another expression for the states of existence: every secondary cycle reproduces, in its own manner, phases corresponding to those of the more extensive cycle to which it is subordinated.

4. Cf. the *Purusha-Sūkta* of the *Rig Veda*, x, 90.

whatever this state may actually be;[5] but this signification, especially if it be a question of the human state (even when taken in the integral development of all its modalities) or of another individual state, is still properly no more than 'cosmological', and what must essentially be considered here is a metaphysical transposition of the idea of individual man, a transposition to be accomplished in the extra-individual and supra-individual domain. In this sense, and if reference is made to what has been said earlier on, the conception of 'Universal Man' will apply in the first place to the sum total of the states of manifestation; but it can be rendered still more universal, in the fullness of the true meaning of that word, if it is also extended to the states of non-manifestation, and hence to the complete and perfect realization of the total being—taking this in the higher sense indicated above, and always with the reservation that the term 'being' itself can then be used in a purely analogical sense only.

It is essential to note here that every metaphysical transposition of the kind just mentioned should be regarded as the expression of an analogy in the rightful sense of the word. To make clear what this implies, we would recall that every true analogy must be applied inversely: this is represented by the well-known symbol of the 'seal of Solomon', formed by the combination of two opposed triangles.[6] For example, just as the image of an object in a mirror is inverted in relation to the object, so that which is the first or greatest in the principial order is, in appearance at least, the last or smallest in the order of manifestation.[7] To take terms of comparison from the mathematical sphere, as we have already done in order to make the matter clearer, the geometrical point is quantitatively nil and occupies no space although (as will be explained later) it is the principle by which the whole of space is produced, the latter being no more than the development or expansion of its virtualities. In the same way, arithmetical unity is the least of numbers when considered as situated among them in their multiplicity, but it is the greatest in

5. On this subject, and in regard to the *Vaishvānara* of the Hindu tradition, see *Man and His Becoming*, chap 12.

6. See ibid., chaps. 1 and 3.

7. We have seen this very clearly expressed in texts taken from both the Upanishads and the Gospel.

principle, since it virtually contains them all and produces the whole series of them by the mere repetition of itself.

There is thus analogy, but not similitude, between individual man—a relative and incomplete being, who is here taken as the type of a certain mode of existence, or even of all conditioned existence—and the total unconditioned being, transcendent in respect of all particular and determined modes of existence, who is symbolically designated as 'Universal Man'. To apply this analogy, it may be said that if 'Universal Man' is the principle of all manifestation, individual man represents, in his own order, its resultant and as it were its end-product, and for this reason all traditions agree in regarding him as being formed by a synthesis of all the elements and all the kingdoms of nature.[8] This must be so if the analogy is to be exact, and so in fact it is; but in order to justify it completely, and with it the very designation 'Universal Man', it would be necessary to go into the question of the cosmogonic function that is peculiar to the human being; to develop this fully would however take us too far afield and we must await another occasion. For the present then suffice it to say that the human being, in the realm of individual existence that pertains to him, plays a part that may truly be described as 'central' in respect of all other beings likewise situated in that realm. By virtue of this part that he plays, man is the most complete expression of the individual state in question, for all its possibilities are as it were integrated in him, at least in a certain respect and on the understanding that they are taken, not in their corporeal modality alone, but in the whole range of all their modalities, with the indefinite extension of which they are capable.[9] Here lie the profoundest of the reasons on which the analogy we are considering rests; and it is this particular situation that allows of a valid

---

8. In this connection we would cite in particular the Islamic tradition regarding the creation of the angels and of men. The real significance of such traditions, needless to say, has absolutely nothing in common with any 'transformist' or even simply 'evolutionist' conception in the most general sense of the word, nor with any of the modern fantasies inspired more or less directly by such anti-traditional conceptions.

9. The realization of the integral human individuality corresponds to the 'primordial state' of which we have often spoken and which is called the 'Edenic state' in the Judeo-Christian tradition.

transposition of the notion of man, rather than of any other manifested being in the same state, in order to transform it into the traditional conception of 'Universal Man'.[10]

One further remark should be added, which is of the first importance: 'Universal Man' exists only virtually, and as it were negatively,
in the manner of an ideal archetype, so long as the effective realization of the total being has not endowed him with actualized positive
existence. This is true for any being whatsoever, when regarded as
carrying out, or destined to carry out, such a realization.[11] To avoid
all misunderstanding, it should be added that such a manner of
speaking, which presents as successive that which is essentially
simultaneous, is valid only insofar as one adopts the special standpoint of a state of manifestation of the being, this state being taken
as a starting-point for the realization. Again, it is clear that expressions such as 'negative existence' and 'positive existence' are not to
be taken literally in contexts where the very notion of 'existence' can
be properly applied only in a certain degree and up to a certain
point; but the imperfections inherent in language, bound up as it is
with the conditions of the human state and even more particularly
with its corporeal and terrestrial modality, often necessitate the use,
with some precautions, of 'verbal images' of this kind, without
which it would be quite impossible to make oneself intelligible,
especially in languages as little adapted to the expression of metaphysical truth as are the Western ones.

10. To forestall misunderstandings, we must recall that we always use the word
'transformation' in its strictly etymological sense, namely that of 'passing beyond
form' and hence beyond all that belongs to the order of individual existence.

11. In a certain sense, the two states, negative and positive, of 'Universal Man'
correspond respectively, in the terminology of the Judeo-Christian tradition, to the
state prior to the 'fall' and the state consequent upon 'redemption'; from this viewpoint, these two states are the two Adams spoken of by Saint Paul (1 Cor 16), which
shows at the same time the relationship of 'Universal Man' to the *Logos* (Cf. *Spiritual Authority and Temporal Power*, chap. 8).

3

METAPHYSICAL
SYMBOLISM OF
THE CROSS

MOST TRADITIONAL DOCTRINES symbolize the realization of 'Universal Man' by a sign that is everywhere the same, because, as was said at the outset, it is one of those directly attached to the primordial tradition. That sign is the sign of the cross, which very clearly represents the manner of achievement of this realization by the perfect communion of all the states of the being, harmoniously and conformably ranked, in integral expansion, in the double sense of 'amplitude' and 'exaltation'.[1] In fact, this double expansion of the being may be regarded as taking place horizontally on the one hand, that is, at a certain given level or degree of existence, and vertically on the other, that is, in the hierarchical superimposition of all the degrees. Thus, the horizontal direction represents 'amplitude' or integral extension of the individuality taken as basis for realization, an extension that consists in the indefinite development of a given group of possibilities subject to certain special conditions of manifestation; and it should be clearly understood that in the case of the human being this extension is in no way confined to the corporeal part of the individuality, but includes all its modalities, of which the

---

1. These terms are borrowed from the language of Islamic esoterism, which is particularly precise on this point. In the Western world, the symbol of the Rose-Cross bore exactly the same meaning, before modern incomprehension gave rise to all kinds of bizarre or insignificant interpretations; the meaning of the rose will be explained later.

corporeal state is properly only one. The vertical direction represents the hierarchy, likewise and *a fortiori* indefinite, of the multiple states, each of which, when similarly considered in its integrality, is one of those groups of possibilities corresponding to one of the 'worlds' or degrees, which are included in the total synthesis of 'Universal Man'.[2] In this cruciform representation, the horizontal expansion therefore corresponds to the indefinitude of possible modalities of one and the same state of the being regarded integrally, and the vertical super-imposition to the indefinite series of states of the total being.

Furthermore, it need hardly be said that the state whose development is depicted by the horizontal line may be any state whatsoever; in fact, it will be the state in which the being that realizes 'Universal Man' is situated in respect of its manifestation, and that state is for such a being the starting-point and the support or basis for this realization. Any and every state can furnish a being with such a basis, as will appear more clearly in what follows; if in this respect more special consideration is accorded to the human state, the reason is that it is our own state and thus concerns us more directly, so that the case we have particularly to deal with is that of beings who start from this state in order to carry out the realization in question; but it should be clearly understood that from the point of view of pure metaphysics this case is in no wise a privileged one.

It may be observed here that the effective totalization of the being, since it is beyond all conditions, corresponds to what the Hindu doctrine calls 'Deliverance' (*Moksha*), and to what Islamic

2. 'When man, in the "universal degree", exalts himself toward the sublime, when there arise in him the other degrees [non-human states] in perfect expansion, he is "Universal Man". Exaltation and amplitude alike have attained their fullness in the Prophet [who is thus identical with "Universal Man"]' (*Epistle on the Manifestation of the Prophet*, by Shaykh Moḥammad ibn Faḍlullah al-Hindī). This will also explain the words uttered about twenty years ago by a personage who then occupied a very high position in Islam: 'If Christians have the sign of the cross, Muslims have the doctrine of it.' We would add that, in the esoteric order, the relationship between 'Universal Man' and the Word on the one hand, and the Prophet on the other, leaves no room, as regards the actual basis of the doctrine, for any real divergence between Christianity and Islam. It would seem that the ancient Persian conception of *Vohu-Mana* also corresponded to that of 'Universal Man'.

esoterism calls the 'Supreme Identity'.[3] Moreover, according to the latter traditional form, 'Universal Man', insofar as he is represented by the couple 'Adam-Eve', has the same number as Allah, which may be taken as a means of expressing the 'Supreme Identity'.[4] This calls for a word of explanation, since it might be objected that the designation 'Adam-Eve', though assuredly capable of transposition, nevertheless applies in its proper sense to the primordial human state alone. Yet if the 'Supreme Identity' is effectively realized only in the totalization of the multiple states, it can still be described as in some sense already virtually realized at the 'Edenic' stage, in the integration of the human being when brought back to his original center, which, as will be shown later, is also the point of direct communication with the other states.[5]

Again, it may be said that the integration of the human state, or of any other state, represents in its own order and degree the actual totalization of the being, as will be made plain by means of the geometrical symbolism that we are about to expound. If this be so, the reason is that it is possible to discover in everything, in individual man for example, or more particularly in corporeal man, a symbol and as it were a figuration of 'Universal Man', since each part of the Universe, whether it be a world or a particular being, is always and everywhere analogous to the whole. Thus a philosopher such as Leibnitz was undoubtedly correct in saying that every 'individual

3. On this subject see the concluding chapters of *Man and His Becoming*.

4. This number, which is 66, is given by the sum of the numerical values of the letters forming the names *Adam wa Ḥawwa*. According to the Hebrew Genesis, man, 'created male and female,' in other words in an androgynic state, is 'in the image of God'; and, following the Islamic tradition, Allah ordered the angels to adore man (Koran II, 34; XVII, 61; XVIII, 50). The original androgynic state is the complete human state, in which the complements, instead of being opposed, are perfectly balanced, a point we shall return to later. Here it need only be added that in the Hindu tradition an expression of this state is to be found symbolically contained in the word *Hamsa*, in which the two complementary poles of the being are made to correspond to the two phases of breathing, which for their part represent the analogous phases of universal manifestation.

5. The two stages here indicated in the realization of the 'Supreme Identity' correspond to the distinction between what might be called 'effective immortality' and 'virtual immortality' (see *Man and His Becoming*, chap. 18).

substance' (with the reservations we have made earlier as to the value of this expression) must contain in itself an integral representation of the Universe, and this is a correct application of the analogy between the 'macrocosm' and the 'microcosm;[6] but in confining himself to the consideration of 'individual substance' and in seeking to equate it with the being itself (a complete and closed being that is to say, lacking any effective communication with anything that transcends it) he debarred himself from passing from the direction of 'amplitude' to that of 'exaltation', and thus deprived his theory of any true metaphysical scope.[7] It is no part of our present intention to enter into the examination of philosophical notions of any kind, or of anything else equally referable to the 'profane' sphere; but the above example came quite naturally to mind as an almost immediate application of what has just been said about the two directions in which the expansion of the total being is carried out.

To return to the symbolism of the cross, it must also be noted that apart from the metaphysical and principial significance so far exclusively spoken of, the cross possesses several other meanings that are more or less secondary and contingent; this is quite normal, following what has been said in general about the plurality of meanings comprised in every symbol. Before developing the geometrical representation of the being and its multiple states, as synthetically contained in the sign of the cross, and before going into details of this symbolism—a rather complex one if developed to its fullest extent—we shall say something about those other meanings; for although the questions connected with them may seem somewhat

6. We have already pointed out that Leibnitz, unlike other modern philosophers in this respect, was in possession of a number of traditional data, which however were fairly elementary and incomplete, and which, to judge by the use he made of them, he does not seem to have completely understood.

7. Another major defect in the conception of Leibnitz, and one that is probably closely bound up with the former, is the introduction of the moral point of view into considerations of a universal order in which it has no place by means of the 'principle of the best', which this philosopher sought to regard as the 'sufficient cause' of all existence. In this connection it should also be pointed out that the distinction between the possible and the real, such as Leibnitz attempted to establish, cannot have any metaphysical value, for all that is possible is thereby also real according to its proper mode.

remote from the real subject of this book, all these things are never-theless linked together in a certain way, and sometimes even more closely than one might be inclined to suppose, always by reason of that law of correspondence which, as explained at the outset, lies at the very foundation of all symbolism.

4

THE DIRECTIONS
OF SPACE

CERTAIN WESTERN WRITERS with more or less initiatic pretensions have sought to read an exclusively astronomical significance into the cross by saying that it is a 'symbol of the cruciform junction that the ecliptic forms with the equator,' and also 'an image of the equinoxes, since the sun successively covers these two points in its annual course.'[1] In fact, if this is so, the reason is, as was mentioned above, that astronomical phenomena themselves can from a higher point of view be regarded as symbols, and as such one may find in them, as in everything else, a figuration of 'Universal Man'. However, if these phenomena are symbols, it is clear that they are not the thing symbolized, and that the fact of confusing the two constitutes a reversal of the normal relationships between different orders of reality.[2] When the figure of the cross is perceived in astronomical or other phenomena, it has exactly the same symbolic value as that which we ourselves can trace;[3] this merely proves that

1. These quotations are taken, as a very typical example, from a well known masonic writer, J.-M. Ragon (*Rituel du grade de Rose-Croix*, pp 25–28).

2. It may be as well to recall here, though we have already done so on many occasions, that this astronomical interpretation, always insufficient in itself and radically false when it seeks to be exclusive, was what gave rise to the notorious 'solar myth' theory, invented in the late eighteenth century by Dupuis and Volnay, later reproduced by Max Müller, and again put forward in our own day by chief representatives of a self-styled 'science of religions', which we find rather difficult to take seriously.

3. It should be noted that symbols always retain their proper value, even when traced without conscious intention, as occurs when certain of them, no longer understood, are preserved merely by way of ornamentation.

true symbolism, far from having been artificially invented by man, is to be found in nature itself, or rather, that the whole of nature amounts to no more than a symbol of the transcendent realities.

Even if we thus restore the correct interpretation of these things, the two sentences just quoted both contain an error. In actual fact, on the one hand, the ecliptic and the equator do not form a cross, for their two planes do not cut at right angles; on the other hand, the two equinoctial points are clearly joined by a straight line, so that here the cross is still less to be seen. What must in reality be considered is, firstly, the plane of the equator and the axis joining the poles and perpendicular to that plane, and then the two lines respectively joining the pair of solstitial points and the pair of equinoctial points; we thus get what might be called, in the first case, the vertical cross, and in the second, the horizontal cross. The combination of the two crosses, which have the same center, forms the three-dimensional cross, the branches of which are oriented in the six directions of space,[4] these latter corresponding to the six cardinal points, which, with the center itself, form the septenary.

We have already remarked elsewhere on the importance that the Eastern doctrines attach to the seven regions of space, and also on their correspondence with certain cyclical periods.[5] It seems worthwhile to reproduce here a text previously quoted, which shows that the same thing is also to be found in the Western traditions: 'Clement of Alexandria says [*Stromateis*, bk. 6, chap. 16] that from God, 'Heart of the Universe', issue all the directions of space, each indefinite in extent, one upward, one downward, one to the right, one to the left, one forward and one backward; turning His gaze in these six directions, none of which extends further than the others, He accomplishes the world; He is the beginning and the end (the *alpha* and *omega*); in Him the six phases of time are accomplished, and

4. 'Directions' and 'dimensions' of space should not be confused: there are six directions but only three dimensions, each of which comprises two diametrically opposed directions. Thus the cross we are considering has six branches, but is formed of only three straight lines, each perpendicular to the other two; in geometrical language, each branch is a 'half-line' running in a certain direction from the center.

5. *The King of the World*, chap. 7.

from Him they receive their indefinite extensions; herein resides the secret of the number seven.'[6]

This symbolism is also that of the Hebrew Kabbalah, which speaks of the 'Holy Palace' or 'Inward Palace' as being situated at the center of the six directions of space. The three letters of the divine name *Jehovah*,[7] by their sextuple permutation in these six directions, indicate the immanence of God in the bosom of the world, that is, the manifestation of the *Logos* at the center of all things in the primordial point, of which all extent is merely the expansion or development: 'Out of the void (*Thohu*) He formed something, and out of that which is not, He made that which is. He carved great columns from the impalpable ether.[8] He reflected, and His Speech (*Memra*) produced every object and all things by His Name, The One.'[9] This primordial point at which the Divine Word is uttered does not develop solely in space, but also in time; it is the 'Center of the World' in every sense, that is, it is at once at the center of space and at the center of time. This, of course, if taken literally, concerns our world alone, being the only one whose conditions of existence are directly expressible in human language; but, as it is really a question of the center of all the worlds, we may pass to the supra-sensible order by making an analogical transposition in which space and time no longer bear any but a purely symbolical meaning.

We have seen that Clement of Alexandria deals with six phases of time, corresponding respectively to the six divisions of space: these, as has been shown, are the six cyclical periods, subdivisions of a more general period, and sometimes represented as six millennia. In fact, both the *Zohar* and the *Talmud* divide the duration of the

---

6. P. Vulliaud, *La Kabbale juive* [Paris: E. Nourry, 1923], vol. I, pp 215–6.

7. This Name is formed of four letters, *iod he vau he*, but there are only three different ones since *he* occurs twice.

8. We are here dealing with the 'columns of the Sephirothic tree'—the central column, the right-hand column, and the left-hand column—of which more will be said later. Again, it is essential to note that the 'ether' here in question should not be understood merely as the first element of the corporeal world, but also in a higher sense obtained by analogical transposition. This applies equally in the case of *Ākāsha* in the Hindu doctrine (see *Man and His Becoming*, chap. 3).

9. *Sepher Yetsirah*, IV, 5.

world into millenary periods: 'The world will endure for six thousand years to which the six first utterances of Genesis allude;[10] and
these six millennia are analogous to the six "days" of Creation.'[11]
The seventh millennium, like the seventh 'day', is the *Sabbath*, that
is, the phase of return to the Principle, which naturally corresponds
to the center, regarded as a seventh region of space. We have here a
sort of symbolical chronology, which must clearly not be taken literally, any more than those found in other traditions: Josephus[12]
remarks that six thousand years form ten 'great years', a 'great year'
being six centuries (the *Naros* of the Chaldeans); but elsewhere what
is denoted by this expression is a far longer period, ten or twelve
thousand years in the case of the Greeks and Persians. This however
does not matter here, since we are in no way trying to calculate the
real duration of our world, which would call for a profound study of
the Hindu theory of *Manvantaras*; it will therefore be enough to
take these divisions with their symbolic value. Accordingly, we will
merely say that we are concerned with six phases of indeterminate
duration, plus a seventh that corresponds to the accomplishment of
all things and their re-establishment in the primal state.[13]

To return to the cosmological doctrine of the Kabbalah as set
forth in the *Sepher Yetsirah*: 'What is in question,' says Vulliaud, 'is a
development proceeding from Thought down to a modification
into Sound (Voice), from the impenetrable to the comprehensible.
It will be seen that we have before us a symbolic account of the mystery that has universal genesis for its object and that is bound up
with the mystery of unity. Other passages give an account of the
"point" that develops by lines in all directions,[14] and that becomes
comprehensible only through the "Inward Palace". It is that "point"
of the ungraspable ether (*Avir*), in which is produced the concentration whence Light (*Aor*) emanates.'[15] The point is in fact the symbol

---

10. *Siphra di-Tseniutha*: *Zohar*, ii, 176B.
11. Cf. the Biblical saying: 'A thousand years are as a day in the sight of our
Lord.'
12. *Antiquities of the Jews* i, 4.
13. This last millennium is doubtless the 'reign of a hundred years' spoken of in
the Apocalypse.
14. These lines are represented as the 'hair of *Shiva*' in the Hindu tradition.
15. *La Kabbale juive*, vol. i, p 217.

of unity; it is the principle of the spatial extent that exists only by its radiation (the previous 'void' being nothing but pure virtuality), but it becomes comprehensible only when one situates oneself in space, of which it is then the center, as will be explained more fully later. The emanation of light, which gives space its reality by 'making something out of the void and that which is out of that which was not,' is an expansion that follows concentration. Here we find the two phases of inspiration and expiration that occur so often in the Hindu doctrine, the second of which corresponds to the production of the manifested world; and one may note the analogy that also exists, in this respect, with the beating of the heart and the circulation of the blood in the living being. But let us proceed: 'The Light (*Aor*) burst forth from the mystery of the ether (*Avir*). The hidden point was manifested, that is to say the letter *yod*.'[16] This letter hieroglyphically represents the Principle, and all the other letters of the Hebrew alphabet are said to be formed from it, a formation which, according to the *Sepher Yetsirah*, symbolizes that of the manifested world itself.[17] It is also said that the incomprehensible primordial point which is the unmanifested One forms from itself three points that represent the Beginning, the Middle, and the End,[18] and that these three points put together constitute the letter *yod*, which is thus the One manifested (or more exactly, affirmed qua principle of universal manifestation), or, to speak in theological terms, God making Himself 'Center of the World' by his Word. 'When this *yod* has been produced,' says the *Sepher Yetsirah*, 'that which remained of the mystery of the hidden *Avir* (ether) was *Aor* (light)'; and in fact, if *yod* is removed from the word *Avir*, what is left is *Aor*.

16. Ibid., vol. I, p 218.

17. This 'formation' (*Yetsirah*) should properly be understood as the production of manifestation in the subtle state; manifestation in the gross state is called *Asiah*, while on the other hand *Beriah* is formless manifestation. For the exact correspondence of the worlds envisaged by the Kabbalah with the *Tribhuvana* of the Hindu doctrine, see *Man and His Becoming*, chap. 5.

18. In this connection these three points can be assimilated to the three elements of the monosyllable *Aum* (*Om*) in the Hindu symbolism, and also in the ancient Christian symbolism (see *Man and His Becoming*, chap. 17, and *The King of the World*, chap. 4).

On this subject Vulliaud quotes the commentary of Moses de
Léon:

After recalling that the Holy One, blessed be He, the Unknow-
able, can be apprehended only through His attributes (*middoth*)
by which He has created the worlds,[19] let us begin with the exege-
sis of the first word of the Torah: Bereshith.[20] Ancient writers
have informed us regarding this mystery that it is hidden in the
Supreme Degree, the pure and impalpable Ether. This degree is
the sum total of all the later mirrors ('later' because they are exterior to that Degree itself).[21] They proceed from it by the mystery
of the point which is itself a hidden degree emanating from the
mystery of the pure mysterious Ether.[22] The first Degree, absolutely concealed (that is to say non-manifested), cannot be
apprehended.[23] Similarly, the mystery of the supreme point,
though profoundly hidden,[24] can be apprehended in the mystery

19. We here find the equivalent of the distinction drawn by the Hindu doctrine
between *Brahma* 'unqualified' (*nirguna*) and *Brahma* 'qualified' (*saguna*), that is,
between the 'Supreme' and the 'Non-Supreme', the latter being not different from
Ishvara (see *Man and His Becoming*, chaps. 1 and 10). *Middah* literally means 'measure' (cf. Sanskrit *Matra*).
20. This, as is well-known, is the opening of Genesis: *In principio....*
21. It is clear that this degree is the same thing as the 'universal degree' of
Islamic esoterism, the one in which all the other degrees—that is, all the states of
Existence—are synthetically totalized. The same doctrine also makes use of the simile of the mirror and others of the same type: thus according to an expression
already quoted elsewhere (*Man and His Becoming*, chap. 10), Unity, considered as
containing in itself all aspects of the Divinity (*asrār rabbāniyyah* or 'dominical mysteries'), that is, all the Divine attributes, expressed by the names *Sifātiyah* (see *The
King of the World*, chap. 3), 'is the reverberating surface of the Absolute (the 'Holy
One' ungraspable apart from His attributes) with countless facets, magnifying
every creature that looks at itself directly therein'; and needless to say it is precisely
these *asrār rabbāniyyah* that are in question here.
22. The degree represented by the point, which corresponds to Unity, is that of
pure Being (*Ishvara* in the Hindu doctrine).
23. In this connection we may refer to the teaching of the Hindu doctrine on
the subject of what is beyond Being, that is, the unconditioned state of *Ātmā* (see
Man and His Becoming, chap. 16, where we have also indicated the concordant
teachings of other traditions).
24. Being is still unmanifested, but is the principle of all manifestation.

THE DIRECTIONS OF SPACE   27

of the inward Palace. The mystery of the Supreme Crown (*Kether*, the first of the ten *Sephiroth*) corresponds to that of the pure and impalpable Ether (*Avir*). It is the cause of all causes and the origin of all origins. It is in this mystery, the invisible origin of all things, that the hidden 'point', whence all proceeds, takes birth. On that account, it is said in the *Sepher Yetsirah*: 'Before One, what canst thou count?' Which means: before that point, what canst thou count or comprehend?[25] Before that point, there was nothing except *Ain*, that is, the mystery of the pure and impalpable Ether, so named (by a simple negation) by reason of its incomprehensibility.[26] The comprehensible beginning of existence lies in the mystery of the supreme 'point'.[27] And since this point is the 'beginning' of all things, it is called 'Thought' (*Mahasheba*).[28] The mystery of creative Thought corresponds to the hidden 'point'. In the inward Palace the mystery attached to the hidden 'point' can be understood, for the pure and impalpable Ether remains forever mysterious. The 'point' is Ether rendered palpable (by the 'concentration' which is the starting-point of all differentiation) in the mystery of the inward Palace or Holy of Holies.[29] Everything, without exception, was at first conceived in Thought.[30] And if anyone should say: 'Lo! there is something new in the world,' impose silence on him, for that

25. One is in fact the first of all numbers; before it, accordingly, nothing that can be counted: here numeration is taken as a symbol of knowledge in distinctive mode.

26. This is the metaphysical Zero, or the 'Non-Being' of the Far-Eastern tradition, symbolized by the 'void' (cf. *Tao Te Ching*, chap. 11); we have already explained elsewhere why expressions of negative form are the only ones still applicable beyond Being (*Man and His Becoming*, chap. 15).

27. That is, in Being, which is the principle of Existence, or in other words universal manifestation, just as unity is the principle and beginning of all numbers.

28. Because all things must be conceived by thought before being realized outwardly; this should be understood analogically by a transposition from the human order to the cosmic.

29. The 'Holy of Holies' was represented by the innermost part of the Temple at Jerusalem, which was the Tabernacle (*miskhan*) wherein the *Shekinah*, that is, the Divine Presence, manifested itself.

30. This is the Word *qua* divine Intellect, which, according to an expression used by Christian theology, is the *locus possibilium*.

thing was previously conceived in Thought.[31] From the hidden 'point' emanates the inward Holy Palace, (by the lines issuing from that point along the six directions of space). This is the Holy of Holies, the fiftieth year (an allusion to the *Jubilee*, which represents the return to the primordial state),[32] which is likewise called the Voice that emanates from Thought.[33] All being and all causes thus emanate by the power of the 'point' from on High. Behold that which relates to the mysteries of the three supreme *Sephiroth*.'[34]

This passage, despite its length, has purposely been quoted in full, because, apart from its own interest, it has a far more direct connection with the subject of the present study than might at first sight be supposed.

The symbolism of the directions of space will be applied in all that follows, whether from the 'macrocosmic' point of view, as in what has gone before, or from the 'microcosmic'. In geometrical terms, the three-dimensional cross forms a 'system of coordinates' to which the whole of space can be referred; here space will symbolize the sum total of all possibilities, either of a particular being or of universal Existence. This system is formed by three axes, one vertical and two horizontal, which are three perpendicular diameters of an indefinite sphere, and which, even independently of any astronomical considerations, may be regarded as oriented toward the six cardinal points. In the text of Clement of Alexandria that has been quoted, upward and downward correspond respectively to the Zenith and the Nadir, right and left to South and North, forward and backward to East and West; confirmation of these correspondences may be found in almost all traditions. It may also be said that

31. This is the 'permanent actuality' of all things in the 'eternal present'.
32. See *The King of the World*, chap. 3; it will be noted that $50 = 7^2 + 1$. The word *kol*, 'all', in Hebrew and Arabic, has the numerical value of 50. Cf. also the 'fifty gates of the Intelligence'.
33. This is still the Word, but *qua* divine Utterance; it is first inward Thought (that is, in Itself), then outward Utterance (that is, in respect of universal Existence), Utterance being the manifestation of Thought; and the first word uttered is the *Yehi Aor* (*Fiat Lux*) of Genesis.
34. *La Kabbale juive*, vol. I, p217.

the vertical axis is the polar axis, that is, the fixed line that joins the two poles and about which all things accomplish their rotation: it is therefore the main axis, whereas the two horizontal axes are only secondary and relative. Of the two latter, the North–South axis may be called the solstitial axis, and the other the equinoctial axis, which brings us back to the astronomical standpoint by virtue of the correspondence between the cardinal points and the phases of the annual cycle. A complete exposition of this correspondence would take us too far afield and is not of consequence here, though a place may perhaps be found for it in another study.[35]

35. Saint Paul alludes to the symbolism of the directions or dimensions of space when he speaks of 'the breadth the length and height and depth' (Eph. 3:18). Here, there are only four terms enunciated distinctly instead of six: the first two correspond respectively to the two horizontal axes, each of the latter being regarded in its totality; the two latter terms correspond to the two halves, upper and lower, of the vertical axis. The reason for this distinction, as regards the two halves of the vertical axis, is that they relate to two different and even in one sense opposed *gunas*; the two complete horizontal axes, on the other hand, relate to one and the same *guna*, as will be made clear in the following chapter.

5

HINDU THEORY
OF THE THREE *GUNAS*

BEFORE GOING ANY FURTHER, and in connection with what has
just been said, it is necessary to refer again to the Hindu theory of
the three *gunas*.[1] Our intention is not to treat this theory in full in
all its applications, but merely to provide a brief summary of it
insofar as it relates to the present subject. The three *gunas* are essential, constitutive, and primordial qualities or attributes of beings
envisaged in their different states of manifestation.[2] They are not
states, but general conditions to which beings are subject—by
which they are bound,[3] as it were—and in which they participate
in indefinitely varying proportions, with the result that they are
distributed hierarchically throughout the entire range of the 'three

---

1. See *Introduction to the Study of the Hindu Doctrines*, pt 2, chap. 11, and *Man
and His Becoming* chap. 4. [See also *Studies in Hinduism*, chap. 4. ED.]

2. The three *gunas* are in fact in *Prakriti* itself, which is the 'root' (*mūla*) of universal manifestation; there, however, they are in perfect equilibrium in their primordial indifferentiation, and all manifestation represents a rupture of that
equilibrium.

3. In its ordinary, literal sense, the word *guna* means 'cord'; similarly, the terms
bandha and *pāsha*, which properly mean 'bond', are applied to all the particular
and limiting conditions of existence (*upādhis*) that more specially define this or
that state or mode of manifestation. It should however be stated that the term *guna*
is applied more particularly to a bowstring; it would thus express, at least in a certain respect, the idea of 'tension' at different degrees, and hence, by analogy, that of
'qualification'; but perhaps it is not so much the idea of 'tension' that is appropriate
here as that of 'tendency', which indeed is akin to it as the words themselves show,
and which is the idea that most closely answers to the definition of the three *gunas*.

worlds' (*Tribhuvana*), that is, throughout all the degrees of universal Existence.

The three gunas are: *sattva*, conformity to the pure essence of Being (*Sat*), which is identical with the light of Knowledge (*jñāna*), symbolized by the luminosity of the heavenly spheres that represent the higher states of the being; *rajas*, the urge that provokes the being's expansion in a given state, in other words the development of those of its possibilities that are situated at a certain level of Existence; lastly, *tamas*, obscurity, assimilated to ignorance (*avidyā*), the dark root of the being considered in its lower states. This is true for all manifested states of the being, but naturally it is also possible to consider these qualities or tendencies more particularly in relation to the human state. Thus *sattva*, the upward tendency, always refers to states that are higher than the particular state taken as basis or starting-point in this hierarchical distribution, and *tamas*, the downward tendency, to states lower than that state; as for *rajas*, it refers to this last state itself, regarded as occupying an intermediate situation between the higher and lower states, and hence defined by a tendency that is neither upward nor downward, but horizontal; in the present case, this is the 'world of man' (*mānava-loka*), that is, the domain or degree of universal Existence occupied by the human individual state. The relationship of all this to the symbolism of the cross will now be readily observed, whether that symbolism is considered from the purely metaphysical or from the cosmological point of view, and whether it is applied to the 'macrocosmic' or to the 'microcosmic' order. In all cases, *rajas* can be said to correspond to the entire horizontal line, or better, if the three-dimensional cross is considered, to the combination of the two lines that define the horizontal plane; *tamas* corresponds to the lower part of the vertical line, that is, the part below the horizontal plane, while *sattva* corresponds to the higher part of this same line, namely the part above the plane in question, which thus divides into two hemispheres, upper and lower, the indefinite sphere mentioned above.

In a Vedic text, the three *gunas* are depicted as turning one into another in ascending order:

All was *tamas* [at the outset of manifestation regarded as emerging from the primordial indifferentiation of *Prakriti*]: It [the
Supreme *Brahma*] commanded a change, and *tamas* took the
hue [that is, the nature][4] of *rajas* [intermediate between darkness and luminosity]; and *rajas*, having received another command, took on the nature of *sattva*.

If we regard the three-dimensional cross as traced out from the center of a sphere, as we have just done and shall often be doing again,
then the change from *tamas* into *rajas* can be represented as the
tracing of the lower half of the sphere, from one pole to the equator,
and that from *rajas* into *sattva* as the tracing of the upper half, from
the equator to the other pole. The imaginary horizontal plane of the
equator then represents, as has been said, the domain of the expansion of *rajas*, whereas *tamas* and *sattva* tend respectively toward the
two poles, the extremities of the vertical axis.[5] Lastly, the point from
which the change of *tamas* into *rajas*, and then that of *rajas* into *sattva*, is ordained, is the actual center of the sphere, as will at once be
clear from what has been said in the previous chapter;[6] this will be
explained more fully later on.[7]

---

4. The word *varna*, which properly means 'color', and by generalization
'quality', is used analogically to denote the nature or essence of a principle or a
being; hence also its use in the sense of 'caste', because the institution of castes,
when its underlying reason is envisaged, essentially translates the diversity of
natures peculiar to different human individuals (see *Introduction to the Study of the
Hindu Doctrines*, pt 3, chap. 6, [also *Studies in Hinduism*, chap. 6. ED.]). The three
gunas, moreover, are actually represented by symbolic colors: *tamas* by black, *rajas*
by red, and *sattva* by white (*Chāndogya Upanishad* vi.3.1; Cf. *Spiritual Authority
and Temporal Power*, chap. 4).

5. This symbolism seems to us to explain and sufficiently justify the image of
the 'bowstring', which is implied in the meaning of the term *guna*.

6. This function of the Principle, in the world and in each being, is what is
referred to by the expression 'inner ruler' (*antar-yāmī*): it directs all things from the
interior, itself residing at the innermost point of all, which is the center (see *Man
and His Becoming*, chap. 14).

7. On this same text considered as providing a diagram of the organization of
the 'three worlds', in correspondence with the three *gunas*, see *The Esoterism of
Dante*, chap. 6.

The above is applicable not only to the degrees of universal Existence but also to the states of any one being; there is always perfect correspondence between these two cases, for each state of a being develops, with all the extension of which it is capable (and which is indefinite), in one given degree of Existence. Again, in the cosmological sphere, it is possible to make certain more particular applications of this theory to the domain of the elements; but as the theory of the elements does not come within the scope of the present study, it is better to reserve everything connected with it for another book in which we intend to deal with the conditions of corporeal existence.

6

THE UNION
OF COMPLEMENTS

WE MUST NOW TURN TO CONSIDER, at least summarily, another aspect of the symbolism of the cross, which is perhaps the one most generally known, although, at first sight at least, it may not seem to have much direct bearing on all that has gone before: we refer to the cross regarded as a symbol of the union of complements. For this purpose it suffices to envisage the cross in the most usual manner, that is to say in its two-dimensional form; to return from that to the three-dimensional form, however, one need only remember that the single horizontal line can be considered as the projection of the entire horizontal plane upon the vertical plane in which the figure is traced. In the present context the vertical line can be taken as representing the active principle, and the horizontal line the passive one. These principles are also respectively designated as masculine and feminine, by analogy with the human order; if they are considered in their widest sense, namely in relation to universal manifestation in its totality, they are then the principles that the Hindu doctrine calls *Purusha* and *Prakriti*.[1] It is not material here to recapitulate or develop the considerations arising out of the relationship between these two principles, but merely to show that despite appearances there is a certain connection between this significance of the cross and what has been called its metaphysical significance.

---

1. See *Man and His Becoming*, chap. 4.

In the first place, while reserving the right to return to the point more explicitly later, we would say that this connection follows from the relationship between the vertical axis and the horizontal plane in the metaphysical signification of the cross. It should be clearly appreciated that terms such as active and passive, or their equivalents, have no meaning except in relation to each other, for complementarism is essentially a correlation between two terms. This being so, it is clear that a complementarism such as that of active and passive can be regarded at different levels, so that one and the same term may play an active or a passive role, according to what it is being placed in correlation with; but in every case it can always be said that in such a relationship the active term is, in its own order, the analogue of *Purusha* and the passive one that of *Prakriti*. Now, it will be seen later that the vertical axis, which connects together all the states of the being by passing through their respective centers, is the locus of manifestation of what the Far-Eastern tradition calls the 'Activity of Heaven'; and this is precisely the 'actionless' activity of *Purusha*, which determines in *Prakriti* the productions that correspond to all the possibilities of manifestation. As for the horizontal plane, it will be seen that this forms a 'plane of reflection', symbolically represented as the 'surface of the waters', and it is well known that in all traditions the 'waters' are a symbol of *Prakriti* or of 'universal passivity'.[2] To be strictly accurate, as this plane represents a certain degree of Existence (and any one of the horizontal planes that correspond to the indefinite multitude of the states of manifestation could be similarly regarded), it is not identified with *Prakriti* itself, but only with something that is already determined by a certain set of special conditions of existence (those which define a world), and that plays the part of *Prakriti* in a relative sense, at a certain level in the scale of universal manifestation.

Another point, which is directly connected with the notion of 'Universal Man', also calls for explanation. We spoke earlier of the latter as being constituted by the couple 'Adam-Eve', and it has been pointed out elsewhere that the couple *Purusha-Prakriti*, either in

2. See ibid, chap. 5.

respect of all manifestation, or more particularly in respect of a given state of being, can be regarded as equivalent to 'Universal Man'.[3] From this point of view, the union of complements must be regarded as constituting the primordial Androgyne of which all traditions speak. Without dwelling further on this point, it can be said that in the totalization of the being, the complements must in fact be in perfect equilibrium, with no predominance of one over the other. Again, it should be noted that the form as a rule symbolically assigned to the Androgyne is the spherical one,[4] which is the least differentiated of all, since it extends equally in all directions, being regarded by the Pythagoreans, for example, as the most perfect form and as the figure of universal totality.[5] In order to represent the idea of totality in this way, it is further necessary, as was said before, that the sphere shall be indefinite in extent, as are the axes that form the cross, which are three perpendicular diameters of this sphere. In other words, as the sphere is constituted by the radiation proceeding from its center, it is never closed, since this radiation is indefinite and fills the whole extent by a series of concentric waves, each of which reproduces the original vibration's two phases of concentration and expansion.[6] These two phases, moreover, are themselves

3. See ibid, chap. 4.

4. In this respect cf. the speech that Plato, in the *Symposium*, puts into the mouth of Aristophanes; most modern commentators have made the mistake of overlooking its symbolical value, obvious though this is. Something quite similar is to be found in a certain aspect of the Far-Eastern symbolism of the *yin-yang*, with which we shall be dealing later.

5. Of all lines of equal length, the circumference is that which encloses the greatest surface; similarly, of all bodies of equal surface, the sphere is that which contains the greatest volume; from the purely mathematical viewpoint this is the reason why these figures were regarded as the most perfect. This idea inspired Leibnitz with his conception of the 'best of worlds', which he defined as being, out of the indefinite multitude of all possible worlds, the one that contains the most being or positive reality; but, as already indicated, the application he made of the idea is devoid of any true metaphysical meaning.

6. This luminous spherical form, not limited and not closed, with its alternations of concentration and expansion (successive from the standpoint of manifestation but in reality simultaneous in the 'eternal present'), is in Islamic esoterism the form of the *Rūḥ muhammadiyah*; it is this total form of Universal Man that God

an expression of complementarism;[7] if we depart from the special conditions inherent in manifestation (in successive mode), and consider them in simultaneity, they balance each other, so that their combination is really equivalent to the principial immutability, just as the sum of the partial disequilibriums by which all manifestation is realized always and invariably constitutes the total equilibrium.

There is one further point that must be mentioned. It was said just now that as the terms active and passive merely express a relationship, they may be applied at different levels; it follows that if we consider the three-dimensional cross, in which the vertical axis and the horizontal plane stand in this active-passive relationship, the same relationship can again be envisaged as between the two horizontal axes, or between what they respectively represent. In this case, in order to preserve the symbolical correspondence established in the first place, and although these axes are both actually horizontal, it is possible to say that one of them - the one that plays the active part - is relatively vertical in respect of the other. For example, if these two axes are regarded as being the solstitial and the equinoctial axis respectively, in accordance with the symbolism of the annual cycle, then the solstitial axis can be described as relatively vertical in relation to the equinoctial, so that in the horizontal plane it plays analogically the part of the polar axis (North-South), and the equinoctial will then play the part of equatorial axis (East-West).[8] Thus in its own plane the horizontal cross reproduces relationships analogous to those expressed by the vertical cross. To return at this point to the metaphysical symbolism, which remains the essentially important one, it can thus be said that the integration

---

commanded the angels to adore; and the reception of this form itself is implied in one of the degrees of Islamic initiation.

7. As indicated above, in the Hindu tradition this is expressed by the symbolism of the word *Hamsa*. In certain Tantric texts there also occurs the word *aha*, symbolizing the union of *Shiva* and *Shakti*, respectively represented by the first and last letters of the Sanskrit alphabet (just as in the Hebrew particle *eth* the *aleph* and the *thau* represent the 'essence' and the 'substance' of a being).

8. This is especially applicable to the symbolism of the *swastika*, which will be discussed later.

of the human state, represented by the horizontal cross, is in its own order of existence a kind of image of the actual totalization of the being, as represented by the vertical cross.[9]

9.   On the subject of complementarism it should also be noted that in the Arabic alphabet the two first letters, *alif* and *ba*, are regarded respectively as active or masculine and as passive or feminine; since the former is vertical in shape and the latter horizontal, their union forms the cross. Again, as the numerical values of these letters are respectively 1 and 2, this agrees with the Pythagorean arithmetical symbolism, according to which the 'monad' is masculine and the 'dyad' feminine. The same concordance is found in the Far-Eastern tradition: in the figures of the *K'ua* or 'trigrams' of Fu Hsi, the *yang* (the masculine principle) is represented by a full line, and the *yin* (the feminine principle) by a broken line (or rather one interrupted in the middle); these symbols, known as the 'two determinations', suggest respectively the ideas of unity and duality; this, needless to say, as in Pythagoreanism itself, should be understood in a sense quite different from that of the mere system of 'numeration' that Leibnitz thought he had discovered in them (see *East and West*, chap. 2). In a general way, according to the *I Ching*, the odd numbers correspond to *yang* and the even numbers to *yin* (see *The Great Triad*, chaps. 4 and 8); the Pythagorean idea of odd and even seems to recur in what Plato calls the 'same' and the 'other', corresponding respectively to unity and duality, envisaged however exclusively in the manifested world. In Chinese numeration, the cross represents the number 10 (and the Roman x indeed is itself only the cross arranged differently); it is here possible to see an allusion to the relationship between the denary and the quaternary: $1 + 2 + 3 + 4 = 10$ in a relationship that was also depicted by the Pythagorean *Tetraktys*. Indeed, in the correspondence of geometrical figures to numbers, the cross naturally represents the quaternary; to be more exact, it represents it under its dynamic aspect, whereas the square represents it under its static aspect. The relation between these two aspects is expressed by the Hermetic problem of the 'squaring of the circle', or, in the symbolism of three-dimensional geometry, by the relation between the sphere and the cube, to which reference has been made in connection with the shapes of the 'Terrestrial Paradise' and the 'Celestial Jerusalem' (*The King of the World*, chap. 11, and *The Reign of Quantity*, chap. 20). Finally, on this subject, it should also be noted that in the number 10 the two digits 1 and 0 further correspond respectively to the active and the passive, represented by the center and the circumference according to another symbolism (see *The Great Triad*, chap. 23), which however can be attached to that of the cross if it is observed that the center is the trace of the vertical axis on the horizontal plane in which the circumference must then be imagined as situated, and the latter will thus represent expansion in this same plane by one of the concentric waves whereby it takes place; the circle with the central point, the figure of the denary, is at the same time the symbol of cyclic perfection, that is, of the integral realization of the possibilities implied in a state of existence.

7

THE RESOLUTION
OF OPPOSITES

THE LAST CHAPTER dealt with complements, not contraries; it is important not to confuse these two notions, as is done at times through taking complementarism for opposition. What may give rise to certain confusions in this respect is that the same things sometimes appear as either contrary or complementary according to the point of view adopted. In such cases, it can always be said that the point of view from which there is opposition is the lower or more superficial one, while that from which there is complementarism, with the opposition reconciled and already resolved, is the higher or profounder point of view, as has been explained elsewhere.[1] The principial unity in fact demands that there shall be no irreducible opposition;[2] accordingly, though opposition between two terms can indeed exist in appearance and can possess a relative reality at a certain level of existence, it is bound to disappear as such and to be harmoniously resolved, by synthesis or integration, when a higher level is attained. To deny this would be to seek to introduce a disequilibrium into the principial order itself, whereas, as was said before, all the disequilibriums that form the elements of manifestation, when they are regarded 'distinctively', are yet bound to concur in the total equilibrium, which nothing can ever affect or destroy. Complementarism itself, which is still duality, must at a certain

---

1. *The Crisis of the Modern World*, chap. 3.
2. Consequently, any 'dualism', whether of the theological order like that attributed to the Manicheans, or of the philosophical order like that of Descartes, is a radically false conception.

degree vanish in face of unity, its two terms being balanced and as it were neutralized when uniting to merge indissolubly in the primordial indifferentiation.

The figure of the cross may make it easier to appreciate the difference between complementarism and opposition. We have seen that the vertical and the horizontal can be taken as representing two complementary terms; but obviously the vertical and the horizontal cannot be said to oppose each other. What do clearly represent opposition, in the same figure, are the contrary directions of the two half-lines from the center which form the two halves of one and the same axis, whichever one it may be; opposition may thus be equally conceived in either the vertical direction or the horizontal. In the vertical two-dimensional cross we shall also have two couples of opposed terms forming a quaternary; the same will be the case in the horizontal cross, one of whose axes may moreover be regarded as relatively vertical, that is, as playing the part of a vertical axis in respect of the other, as was explained at the end of the last chapter. If the two figures are combined to form the three-dimensional cross, we get three pairs of opposed terms, as has already been shown in connection with the directions of space and the cardinal points. It should be noted that one of the best-known quaternary oppositions, namely that of the elements and their corresponding sensible qualities, can properly be disposed as a horizontal cross; in this case, in fact, what is involved is solely the constitution of the corporeal world, which is entirely situated at one single degree of Existence and represents only a quite restricted portion of that. The same holds good when we consider only four cardinal points, which are then those of the terrestrial world, symbolically represented by the horizontal plane, whereas the Zenith and the Nadir, being opposed along the vertical axis, represent an orientation toward worlds that are respectively higher and lower than the terrestrial world. We have seen that this is likewise true for the double opposition of the solstices and the equinoxes, and this also is easy to understand, for the vertical axis, remaining fixed and motionless while all things rotate around it, is obviously independent of cyclic vicissitudes, which it thus governs as it were by its very immobility, the latter being an image of the principial immutability (this is Aristotle's 'unmoved mover', to which we have often referred). If the horizontal cross alone is considered, the vertical axis is there represented by the central point itself, which is the point at which this axis meets the horizontal plane; thus, in every horizontal plane, symbolizing a state or degree of Existence, this point—which may be called its center since it is the origin of the system of coordinates to which every point in the plane can be referred—presents likewise an image of immutability If this rule is applied, for instance, to the theory of the elements of the corporeal world, the center will correspond to the fifth element, namely ether,[3] which is in reality the first of all in the order of production, the one from which all the others proceed by successive differentiation, and the one that combines in itself all the opposing qualities that mark the other elements, in a state of indifferentiation and perfect equilibrium, corresponding in its own order to the principial non-manifestation.[4]

At the center of the cross, therefore, all oppositions are reconciled and resolved; that is the point where the synthesis of all contrary terms is achieved, for in reality they are contrary only from the outward and particular points of view of knowledge in distinctive mode. This central point corresponds to what Islamic esoterism calls the 'Divine station', namely 'that which combines contrasts and antinomies' (al-maqām lillahi huwa maqām ijtimā 'al-ḍiddāin;[5] in

---

3. This is the 'quintessence' (quinta essentia) of the alchemists, sometimes represented, in the center of the cross of the elements, by a figure such as a five-pointed star or a five-petalled flower. It is also said that ether has a 'fivefold nature'; this should be understood of ether considered in itself and as principle of the other four elements.

4. It is for these reasons that the term 'ether' lends itself to the analogical transpositions pointed out earlier; it is then taken symbolically as a designation of the principial state itself.

5. This 'station', or degree of the being's effective realization, is attained by al-fanā', that is, by the 'extinction' of the ego in the return to the 'primordial state'; such 'extinction' even as regards the literal meaning of the term denoting it, is not without analogy to the Nirvāna of the Buddhist doctrine. Beyond al-fanā', there is still fanā' al-fanā', the 'extinction of the extinction', which similarly corresponds to Parinirvāna (see Man and His Becoming, chap. 13). In a certain sense, the passage from one of these degrees to the other is related to the identification of the center of a state of the being with that of the total being, as will be explained later.

the Far-Eastern tradition, it is called the 'Invariable Middle' (*Ching-Ying*), which is the place of perfect equilibrium, represented as the center of the 'cosmic wheel',[6] and is also, at the same time, the point where the 'Activity of Heaven' is directly manifested.[7] This center directs all things by its 'actionless activity' (*wei wu-wei*), which although unmanifested, or rather because it is unmanifested, is in reality the plenitude of activity, since it is the activity of the Principle whence all particular activities are derived; this has been expressed by Lao Tzu as follows: 'The Principle is always actionless, yet everything is done by It.'[8]

According to the Taoist doctrine, the perfect sage is he who has arrived at the central point and abides there in indissoluble union with the Principle, sharing Its immutability and imitating Its 'actionless activity': 'He who has reached the maximum of emptiness,' says Lao Tzu also, 'shall be fixed steadfastly in repose.... To return to one's root [that is, to the Principle, at once the first origin and last end of all beings],[9] is to enter into the state of repose.'[10] The 'emptiness' here in question is complete detachment from all manifested, transitory, and contingent things;[11] by it the being escapes from the vicissitudes of the 'current of forms', from the alternation of the states of 'life' and 'death' or of 'condensation' and 'dissipation',[12] and passes from the circumference of the 'cosmic wheel' to its center, itself described as 'the void [the unmanifest] which unites

6. See *The King of the World*, chaps. 1 and 4, and *The Esoterism of Dante*, chap. 8.

7. Confucianism develops the idea of the 'Invariable Middle' in the social order, whereas its purely metaphysical meaning is given by Taoism.

8. *Tao Te Ching*, chap. 37.

9. The word *Tao*, literally 'Way', which denotes the Principle, is represented by an ideographic character combining the signs for the head and the feet, and equivalent to the symbol of *alpha* and *omega* in the Western traditions.

10. *Tao Te Ching*, chap. 16.

11. This detachment is identical with *al-fanā*; compare also the teaching of the *Bhagavad-Gītā* on indifference toward the fruits of action, by which indifference the being escapes the indefinite chain of the action's results: this is 'action without desire', whereas 'action with desire' (*sakāma karma*) is action carried out with a view to its fruits.

12. Aristotle, in a similar sense, speaks of 'generation' and 'corruption'.

the spokes and makes them into a wheel.'[13] 'Peace in emptiness,' says
Lieh Tzu, 'is an undefinable state; it is neither taken nor given; one
comes to be established therein.'[14] This 'peace in emptiness' is the
'Great Peace' of Islamic esoterism,[15] called in Arabic *as-Sakīnah*, a
designation which identifies it with the Hebrew *Shekinah*, that is,
the Divine Presence at the center of the being, symbolically represented as the heart in all traditions.[16] This Divine Presence is in fact
implied by union with the Principle, which cannot be effectively
attained except at the very center of the being.

To him that dwells in the Unmanifest, all beings manifest
themselves.... United with the Principle, he is thereby in harmony with all beings. United with the Principle, he knows all
through general reasons of a higher order, and consequently no
longer uses his various senses to know in particular and in detail.
The true reason of things is invisible, ungraspable, undefinable,

13. *Tao Te Ching*, chap. 11. The simplest form of the wheel is the circle divided
into four equal parts by the cross; apart from this four-spoked wheel, the most
widespread forms in the symbolism of all peoples are the six- and eight-spoked
wheels; naturally each of these numbers adds a particular nuance to the general significance of the wheel. The octagonal figure of the eight *K'ua* or 'trigrams' of Fu
Hsi, one of the fundamental symbols of the Far-Eastern tradition, is in some
respects equivalent to the eight-spoked wheel, as also to the eight-petalled lotus. In
the ancient traditions of Central America, the world is always symbolized by a circle with a cross inscribed in it.

14. *Lieh Tzu*, chap. 1. The texts of Lieh Tzu and of Chuang Tzu are quoted from
the French translation of Father Wieger.

15. This is also the *Pax Profunda* of the Rosicrucian tradition.

16. See *Man and His Becoming*, chap. 13, and *The King of the World*, chap. 3. It is
said that Allah 'makes peace descend into the hearts of the faithful' (*Huwa alladhī
anzala al-sakīnata fī qulūb al-mu'minīn*): and the Hebrew Kabbalah teaches exactly
the same thing: 'The *Shekinah* bears this name,' says the Hebraist Louis Cappel,
'because it dwells (*shakan*) in the heart of the faithful, which habitation was symbolized by the Tabernacle (*Mishkan*) where God is deemed to reside' (*Critica sacra*,
g311, Amsterdam 1689, quoted by P. Vulliaud, *La Kabbale juive*, vol. I, p 293). It need
hardly be pointed out that the 'descent' of 'Peace' into the heart takes place down
the vertical axis: it is the manifestation of the 'Activity of Heaven'. See also, on the
other hand, the teaching of the Hindu doctrine on the dwelling of *Brahma*, symbolized by ether, in the heart, that is, at the vital center of the human being (*Man
and His Becoming*, chap. 3).

indeterminable. Only the spirit re-established in the state of perfect simplicity can attain it in profound contemplation.[17]

Placed at the center of the 'cosmic wheel', the perfect sage moves it invisibly[18] by his mere presence, without sharing in its movement and without having to concern himself with exercising any action whatever: 'The ideal is the indifference [detachment] of the transcendent man, who lets the cosmic wheel turn.'[19] This absolute detachment renders him the master of all things, because, having passed beyond all oppositions inherent in multiplicity, he can no longer be affected by anything:

He has attained perfect impassibility; life and death are equally indifferent to him, the collapse of the [manifested] universe would cause him no emotion.[20] By dint of search, he has reached

17. *Lieh Tzu*, chap. 4. This shows the whole difference between the transcendent knowledge of the sage and ordinary or 'profane' learning; allusions to 'simplicity', an expression of the unification of all the powers of the being, and regarded as characteristic of the 'primordial state', are frequent in Taoism. Similarly, in the Hindu doctrine, the state of 'childhood' (*bālya*), taken in the spiritual sense, is regarded as a preliminary condition for acquiring true knowledge (see *Man and His Becoming*, chap. 23). In this connection we may recall the similar sayings to be found in the Gospel: 'Truly, I say to you, whoever does not receive the Kingdom of God as a child shall not enter it' (Luke 18:17); 'thou hast hidden these things from the wise and understanding and have revealed them to babes' (Matt. 11:25; Luke 10:21). The central point, whereby communication with the higher or 'heavenly' states is established, is the 'strait gate' of the Gospel symbolism; the 'rich' who cannot enter are the beings attached to multiplicity, and consequently incapable of raising themselves from distinctive to unified knowledge. 'Spiritual poverty', which is detachment in regard to manifestation, here appears as another symbol equivalent to that of 'childhood': 'Blessed are the poor in spirit, for theirs is the kingdom of heaven' (Matt. 10:3). This 'poverty' (in Arabic *al-faqr*) likewise plays an important part in Islamic esoterism; apart from what has just been said, it also implies the being's complete dependence, in all that it is, on the Principle, 'outside of which there is nothing, absolutely nothing that exists' (Muḥyi 'd-Dīn ibn al-'Arabī, *Risālat-al-Aḥadiyah*).

18. The same idea is expressed in the Hindu tradition by the term *Chakravartī*, literally 'he who makes the wheel to turn' (see *The King of the World* chap. 2, *The Esoterism of Dante*, chap. 7, and *The Reign of Quantity*, chap. 39).

19. *Chuang Tzu*, chap. 1. Cf. *The King of the World*, chap. 9.

20. Despite the apparent resemblance of certain expressions, this 'impassibility' is quite different from that of the Stoics, which was solely of a 'moral' order, and moreover seems to have never been more than a mere theoretical conception.

the immutable truth, the unique universal Principle. He lets all beings evolve according to their destinies, and himself stands at the motionless center of all destinies. . . .[21] The outward sign of this inner state is imperturbability: not that of the hero who hurls himself alone, for love of glory, against an army in line of battle, but that of the spirit which, higher than heaven, earth and all beings,[22] dwells in a body to which it is indifferent,[23] taking no account of what its senses convey to it, and knowing all by global knowledge in its motionless unity.[24] That spirit, absolutely independent, is the master of men; if he cared to call them all together in their multitude, they would all rally on the appointed day; but he has no desire for their service.[25]

At the central point, all oppositions inherent in more external points of view are transcended; all oppositions have disappeared and are resolved in a perfect equilibrium.

In the primordial state, these oppositions did not exist. They are derived from the diversification of beings [inherent in manifestation and contingent like it], and from their contacts caused by the universal gyration.[26] They would cease, if the diversity and the movement ceased. They cease forthwith to affect the being who has reduced his distinct ego and his particular movement to

21. According to the traditional commentary on the *I Ching* 'the word 'destiny' denotes the true raison d'être of things'; the 'center of all destinies' is thus the Principle inasmuch as all beings have in it their sufficient cause.

22. The Principle or 'Center', in fact, is prior to all distinction, including that of 'Heaven' (*T'ien*) and 'Earth' (*Ti*), which represents the first duality, these two terms being the equivalents of *Purusha* and *Prakriti* respectively.

23. This is the *jîvan-mukta* (see *Man and His Becoming*, chap. 24).

24. Cf. the condition of *Prâjna* in the Hindu doctrine (ibid., chap. 15).

25. *Chuang-Tzu*, chap. 5. The independence of one who, detached from all contingent things, has arrived at knowledge of the immutable truth, is likewise affirmed by the Gospel: '. . . and you shall know the truth, and the truth will make you free' (John 8:31). One might also find a parallel with the above in another Gospel saying: 'But seek first his kingdom and his righteousness, and all these things will be yours as well' (Matt 6:33; Luke 12:31). Here we must remember the close connection between the idea of justice and those of balance and harmony; for the relationship that unites justice and peace, see *The King of the World*, chaps. 1 and 6 and *Spiritual Authority and Temporal Power*, chap. 8.

26. That is, by rotation of the 'cosmic wheel' about its axis.

almost nothing.[27] Such a being no longer comes into conflict with any other being, because he is established in the infinite, effaced in the indefinite.[28] He has reached the starting-point of all transformations, the neutral point at which there are no conflicts, and there he abides. By concentration of his nature, by nourishment of his vital spirit, by re-assembly of all his powers, he is united to the principle of all births. His nature being whole [synthetically totalized in the principial unity], his vital spirit being intact, no being can harm him.[29]

This central, primordial point is identical with the 'Holy Palace' of the Hebrew Kabbalah; in itself it has no situation, for it is wholly independent of space, which is merely the result of its expansion or indefinite development in every direction, and which accordingly proceeds entirely from it: 'Let us but transport ourselves in spirit outside this world of dimensions and localizations, and there will no longer be need to seek the abode of the Principle.'[30] But once space is realized, the primordial point, while always remaining essentially 'unlocalized' (for it cannot be affected or modified by anything whatsoever), makes itself the center thereof (that is to say, transposing the symbolism, the center of universal manifestation), as we have already shown. From this point start the six directions, which, as pairs of opposites, represent all contraries, and to it also they return, by the alternating movements of expansion and contraction which constitute the two complementary phases of all manifestation. It is the second of these phases, the movement of

27. This reduction of the 'distinct ego', which finally disappears by reabsorbing itself into one single point, is the same thing as the 'emptiness', referred to earlier; it is also the *al-fanā'* of Islamic esoterism. It is clear from the symbolism of the wheel that the 'movement of a being becomes less and less the nearer he approaches to the center'.

28. The first of these expressions refers to the 'personality' and the second to the 'individuality'.

29. *Chuang Tzu*, chap. 19. The last sentence again refers to the conditions of the 'primordial state': it is what the Judeo-Christian tradition denotes as the immortality of man before the 'fall', an immortality regained by him who reaches the 'Center of the World' and eats of the 'Tree of Life'.

30. Idem., chap. 22.

return toward the origin, that marks the way followed by the sage to reach union with the Principle: the 'concentration of his nature', the 're-assembly of all his powers', in the text just quoted, indicate this as clearly as possible; and the 'simplicity' to which reference has also been made corresponds to the unity 'without dimensions' of the primordial point. 'The absolutely simple man sways all beings by his simplicity ... so that nothing opposes him in the six regions of space, nothing is hostile to him, and fire and water do not harm him.'[31] In fact, he stands at the center, from which the six directions have issued by radiation, and on returning to which they become neutralized, so that at this unique point their threefold opposition ceases entirely and nothing that springs therefrom or resides therein can touch the being who dwells there in immutable unity. Opposing nothing, he can likewise be opposed by nothing, for opposition is necessarily a reciprocal relationship, which requires the presence of two terms and is therefore incompatible with the principial Unity; and hostility, which is only a consequence or an outward manifestation of opposition, cannot exist toward a being who is beyond all opposition. Fire and water, types of contraries in the 'elemental world', cannot harm him, for in truth they no longer exist for him *qua* contraries, since by balancing and neutralizing each other by a union of their apparently opposed but really complementary qualities,[32] they have re-entered the indifferentiation of the primordial ether.

For the being who stands at the center, all is unified, for he sees all in the unity of the Principle. All particular (or if preferred, 'particularist') and analytical viewpoints, which are founded only on contingent distinctions and which give rise to all the divergence of individual opinions, have disappeared for him and are reabsorbed into the total synthesis of transcendent knowledge, which is the same as the one and changeless truth. 'His viewpoint is one at which

31. *Lieh Tzu*, chap. 2.
32. Fire and water, envisaged no longer under the aspect of opposition but under that of complementarism, are one of the expressions of the two principles, active and passive, in the domain of corporeal or sensible manifestation; the considerations relating to this viewpoint have been more especially developed by Hermeticism.

this and that, yes and no, appear still in a state of non-distinction. This point is the Pivot of the Law; it is the motionless center of a circumference on the rim of which all contingencies, distinctions, and individualities revolve; and from it only Infinity is to be seen, which is neither this nor that, nor yes nor no. To see all in the yet undifferentiated primordial unity, or from such a distance that all melts into one, this is true intelligence.'[33] The 'Pivot of the Law' is what almost all traditions refer to as the 'Pole',[34] that is, as has already been explained, the fixed point around which all the revolutions of the world are accomplished and which is itself the direct emanation of the center, in other words the expression in the cosmic order[35] of the 'Will of Heaven'.

33. *Chuang Tzu*, chap. 2.

34. We have studied this symbolism particularly in *The King of the World*. In the Far-Eastern tradition, the 'Great Unity' (*Tai-i*) is represented as residing in the pole star which is called *Tien-ki*, that is, literally 'roof of Heaven'.

35. 'Uprightness' (*Te*), whose name recalls the idea of the straight line, and more particularly that of the 'World Axis', is, in the doctrine of Lao Tzu, what might be called a 'specification' of the 'Way' (*Tao*), in regard to a given being or state of existence: it is the direction that being must follow in order that its existence may be according to the 'Way', or, in other words, in conformity with the Principle (in the upward direction, whereas the descending direction is that in which the 'Activity of Heaven' is exerted). This may be compared with what we have indicated elsewhere (*The King of the World*, chap. 8) on the subject of ritual orientation, with which we shall deal again later. [Cf. also *The Great Triad*, chap. 7. ED.]

8

WAR AND PEACE

WHAT HAS JUST BEEN SAID about the 'peace' that dwells at the central point, brings us to another symbolism, namely that of war, to which some allusions have already been made elsewhere.[1] A well-known example of this symbolism is found in the *Bhagavad-Gītā*; the battle described in that book represents action in a quite general sense, and in a form suited to the nature and function of the Kshatriyas for whom it is more particularly intended.[2] The battlefield (*kshetra*) is the domain of action in which the individual develops his possibilities; it is depicted by the horizontal plane in the geometrical symbolism. Here, the human state is in question, but the same representation could be applied to any other state of manifestation equally subject, either to action properly so called, or at least to change and multiplicity. This conception is not peculiar to the Hindu doctrine, but is also found in the Islamic, for this is the real meaning of 'holy war' (*jihād*). The social and outward application is only secondary, as clearly appears from the fact that it is referred to

1. *The King of the World*, chap. 10; *Spiritual Authority and Temporal Power*, chaps. 3 and 8.

2. Krishna and Arjuna, who represent the 'Self' and the 'ego', or the 'personality' and the 'individuality', *Ātmā* unconditioned and *jīvātmā*, are riding in the same chariot, which is the 'vehicle' of the being when considered in its state of manifestation. While Arjuna fights, Krishna drives the chariot without fighting, in other words without himself being engaged in action. Other symbols having a similar meaning are found in several texts of the *Upanishads*: the 'two birds who dwell on the same tree' (*Mundaka Upanishad* III.1.1; *Shvetāshvatara Upanishad* IV.6) and also 'the two who have entered the cave' *Katha Upanishad* I.3.1. The 'cave' is the same thing as the cavity of the heart, which represents the place of union of the individual with the Universal, or of the 'ego' with the 'Self' (see *Man and His Becoming*, chap. 3). In the same sense, Al-Ḥallāj says: 'We are two spirits conjoined in one and the same body' (*naḥnu rūḥān ḥalalnā badanan*).

only as the 'lesser holy war' (*al-jihād al-aṣghar*), whereas the 'greater holy war' (*al-jihād al-akbar*) is of a purely inward and spiritual order.[3]

From whatever aspect and in whatever domain war is envisaged, one may say that the essential reason for its existence is to put a stop to disorder and to restore order. In other terms, it is concerned with the unification of multiplicity by means which belong to the world of multiplicity itself; in this light, and in this light alone, can war be regarded as legitimate. Disorder is in a sense inherent in all manifestation, for manifestation, considered apart from its principle, that is to say as non-unified multiplicity, is nothing but an indefinite series of ruptures of equilibrium. Accordingly, if war is understood in this sense, and is not given an exclusively human meaning, it represents a cosmic process whereby what is manifested is re-integrated into the principial unity; that is why, from the viewpoint of manifestation itself, this reintegration appears as a destruction, and this emerges very clearly from certain aspects of the symbolism of *Shiva* in the Hindu doctrine.

If it be argued that war itself is also a disorder, this is true in a certain respect, and even necessarily true by the very fact that war is waged in the world of manifestation and multiplicity. But it is a disorder intended to balance another disorder, and according to the teaching of the Far-Eastern tradition, previously mentioned, it is the sum of all disorders or disequilibriums that constitutes the total order. Furthermore, order only appears when a standpoint is taken that is above multiplicity and from which things are no longer seen in isolation and 'distinctively', but in their essential unity. This is the standpoint of reality, for apart from its principle multiplicity has only an illusory existence; but that illusion, with the disorder inherent in it, endures for every being so long as it has not arrived in a fully effective manner (and not merely theoretically) at this standpoint of the 'unity of Existence' (*Waḥdat al-wujūd*) in all the modes and degrees of universal manifestation.

---

3. This rests on a *hadīth* of the Prophet, who, on returning from a war-like expedition, spoke as follows: 'We have returned from the lesser holy war to the greater holy war' (*rajaʻnā min al-jihād al-asghar ilā al-jihād al-akbar*).

Accordingly, the end of war is the establishment of peace, for peace, even taken in its most ordinary sense, is ultimately nothing else but order, equilibrium, or harmony, these three terms being practically synonymous, and all denoting under somewhat different aspects the reflection of unity in multiplicity. In point of fact, multiplicity is not really destroyed but 'transformed'; and when all things are brought back to unity, this unity appears in all things, which, far from ceasing to exist, thereby acquire on the contrary the plenitude of reality. In this way, the two complementary viewpoints of 'unity in multiplicity and multiplicity in unity' (*al-waḥdah fil-kathrah wa'l-kathrah fī āl-waḥdah*) are indivisibly united at the central point of all manifestation, which is the 'Divine Abode' or 'Divine Station' (*al-maqām al-ilāhī*), already mentioned above. For whoever has reached that point, there are no longer any contraries, and therefore no longer any disorder; it is the seat of order, of equilibrium, and of harmony or peace; outside of it, for one who is merely striving toward it without having yet reached it, there prevails a state of war such as we have described, since the oppositions in which disorder resides have not yet been permanently transcended.

Even in its outward and social sense, legitimate war, which is waged against the disturbers of order and is aimed at reimposing order upon them, is essentially a function of 'justice', or in other words a 'balancing' function,[4] whatever the secondary and transient appearances may suggest; but this is only the 'lesser holy war', which is a mere image of the other, the 'greater holy war'. Here we would refer to what we have said regarding the symbolical value of historical facts, which can be regarded as representing in their own sphere realities of a higher order.

The 'greater holy war' is man's struggle against the enemies he carries within himself, that is, against the elements in him that are opposed to order and unity. There is however no question of annihilating these elements, which, like everything that exists, have their reason for existence and their place in the whole; what is aimed at is to 'transform' them, by bringing them back and as it were reabsorbing them into unity. Above all else, man must constantly strive

4. See *The King of the World*, chap. 6.

to realize unity in himself, in all that constitutes him, through all the modalities of his human manifestation: unity of thought, unity of action, and also, which is perhaps hardest, unity between thought and action. As regards action, it is important to observe that it is the intention (*niyyah*) which counts for most, for this alone depends wholly on man himself, without being affected or modified by outward contingencies as the results of action always are. Unity in intention and the constant tendency toward the invariable and immutable center[5] are symbolically represented by ritual orientation (*qiblah*), the earthly spiritual centers being as it were visible images of the true and only center of all manifestation. This center, as already explained, has its direct reflection in all the worlds, at the central point of each of them, and also in all beings, in whom this central point is symbolically denoted as the heart, because of its correspondence to the heart in the bodily organism.

For whoever has achieved the perfect realization of unity in himself, all opposition has ceased and with it the state of war, for from the standpoint of totality, which lies beyond all particular standpoints, nothing remains but absolute order. Nothing can thereafter harm such a one, since for him there are no longer any enemies, either within him or without; the unity achieved within is also reflected outwardly, or rather, there is no longer in this case either 'within' or 'without', since this is simply one of the oppositions which 'vanish at his glance'.[6] Permanently established at the center of all things, he 'is unto himself his own law',[7] because his will is one with the universal Will (the 'Will of Heaven' of the Far-Eastern tradition, which effectively manifests itself at the very point where that being resides); he has obtained the 'Great Peace', which is none

---

5. With regard to 'right intention' and 'good will', see *The King of the World*, chaps. 3 and 8.

6. This 'glance', according to the Hindu tradition, is that of the third eye of *Shiva*, which represents the 'sense of eternity', and the effective possession of which is essentially implied in the restoration of the 'primordial state' (see *Man and His Becoming*, chap. 20, and *The King of the World*, chaps. 5 and 7).

7. This expression is borrowed from Islamic esoterism; in the same sense, the Hindu doctrine speaks of the being who has reached that state as *svechchachâri*, that is, 'accomplishing his own will'.

other than the 'Divine Presence' (*as-Sakīnah*), the immanence of the Divinity at that point which is the 'Center of the World'; being identified, by his own unification, with the principial unity itself, he sees unity in all things and all things in unity, in the absolute simultaneity of the Eternal Present.

9

THE TREE
IN THE MIDST

ANOTHER ASPECT OF the symbolism of the cross identifies it with what various traditions describe as the 'Tree in the Midst' or some equivalent term. It has been shown elsewhere that this tree is one of the numerous symbols of the 'World Axis'.[1] It is therefore the vertical line of the cross, which represents this axis, that we must chiefly consider here; this line forms the trunk of the tree, whereas the horizontal line (or the two horizontal lines in the case of the three-dimensional cross) forms its branches. This tree stands at the center of the world, or rather of a world, that is, of a domain in which a state of existence, such as the human state, is developed. In biblical symbolism, for example, the 'Tree of Life', planted in the midst of the Terrestrial Paradise, represents the center of our world, as has been explained on other occasions.[2] Although we have no intention of examining the symbolism of the tree in all its aspects, there are nevertheless a number of points connected with it which are relevant to the present subject.

In the Terrestrial Paradise, there was not only the 'Tree of Life'. There was another tree which plays a no less important and even better known part, namely the 'Tree of the Knowledge of good and evil'.[3] It is said that the latter tree was likewise 'in the midst of the

---

1. *The King of the World*, chap. 2; on the 'World Tree' and its different forms, see also *Man and His Becoming*, chap. 5. In Islamic esoterism, there is a treatise by Muḥyi 'd-Dīn ibn al-'Arabī entitled *The World Tree (Shajarat al-kawn)*.

2. *The King of the World*, chaps. 5 and 9; *Spiritual Authority and Temporal Power*, chaps. 5 and 8.

3. On the vegetable symbolism in relation to the Terrestrial Paradise, see *The Esoterism of Dante*, chap. 9, and *The Reign of Quantity*, chap. 20.

garden';[4] and finally, after having eaten of the fruit of the 'Tree of Knowledge',[5] Adam would only have had to stretch out his hand to take also of the fruit of the 'Tree of Life'.[6] In the second of these three passages, the ban imposed by God relates solely to 'the tree which is in the midst of the garden,' which is not otherwise specified; but if we refer to the other passage where the ban has already been imposed,[7] we see that it is clearly the 'Tree of the Knowledge of good and evil' which is meant in both cases. It is doubtless the bond established by this proximity that causes the two trees to be closely united in symbolism; in fact certain emblematic trees have features that recall both trees at once; but it remains to explain in what this bond consists.

The nature of the 'Tree of the Knowledge of good and evil', as its name implies, is characterized by duality, for in this name there are two terms which are not even complementary but in truth opposed; indeed, it can be said that their whole raison d'être lies in this opposition, for once it is transcended there can no longer be any question of good or evil. The same cannot be said of the 'Tree of Life', which on the contrary, in its function of 'World Axis', essentially implies unity. Accordingly, whenever one finds an image of duality in a tree, the implication is that the 'Tree of Knowledge' is being alluded to, even though in other respects the symbol considered may undeniably be a figure of the 'Tree of Life'. This is so, for instance, with the 'Sephirothic tree' of the Hebrew Kabbalah, which is expressly termed the 'Tree of Life', yet in which the 'right-hand column' and the 'left-hand column' provide a representation of duality; but between the two stands the 'middle column', in which the two opposing tendencies are balanced, and the unity of the 'Tree of Life' thus restored.[8]

4. Gen. 2:9.
5. Ibid., 3:3.
6. Ibid., 3:22.
7. Ibid., 2:17.
8. On the subject of the 'Sephirothic tree', see *The King of the World*, chap. 3. Similarly, in medieval symbolism, the 'tree of the living and the dead', with its two sides whose fruits represent good and bad works respectively, clearly resembles the 'Tree of the Knowledge of good and evil'; while its trunk, which is Christ himself, identifies it with the 'Tree of Life'.

The dual nature of the 'Tree of Knowledge' moreover appears to Adam only at the very moment of the 'Fall', since it is then that he becomes 'knowing good and evil.'[9] It is then too that he finds himself driven out from the center which is the place of the primal unity to which the Tree of Life corresponds; and it is precisely 'lest he put forth his hand and take also of the Tree of Life' that the Cherubim ('tetramorphs' synthesizing the quaternary of elemental powers), armed with flaming swords, are set at the entrance to Eden.[10] This center has become inaccessible to fallen man, who has lost the 'sense of eternity', which is also the 'sense of unity';[11] to return to the center by the restoration of the primordial state, and to reach the 'Tree of Life', is to regain the 'sense of eternity'.

Moreover, we know that the cross of Christ is itself symbolically identified with the 'Tree of Life' (*lignum vitae*), for reasons that are readily understandable; but according to a 'legend of the Cross' current in the Middle Ages, the cross was made of the wood of the 'Tree of Knowledge', so that the latter, after being the instrument of the Fall, thus became that of the Redemption. Here we find expressed a connection between the two ideas of 'fall' and 'redemption' which are in some respects opposed to each other, and there is also an allusion to the re-establishment of the primordial state;[12] in this new guise, the 'Tree of Knowledge' is in a certain sense assimilated to the 'Tree of Life', duality being effectively reintegrated into unity.[13]

9. Gen. 3:22. When 'the eyes of both were opened,' Adam and Eve covered themselves with fig-leaves (ibid., 3:7). It may be noted that in the Hindu tradition the 'World Tree' is represented by the fig; the part that the same tree plays in the Gospel will also be remembered.

10. Ibid., 3:22.

11. Cf. *The King of the World*, chap. 5.

12. This symbolism is connected with what Saint Paul says of the two Adams (1 Cor. 15). The depiction of Adam's skull at the foot of the cross, after a legend according to which he was buried at Golgotha itself ('the place of the skull'), is only another symbolic expression of the same relationship.

13. It is noteworthy that the cross, in its ordinary form, is found in Egyptian hieroglyphs where it has the meaning of 'health' (for instance in the name of Ptolemy *Soter*). This sign is quite distinct from the *crux ansata* or the 'looped cross' (*ankh*), which for its part expresses the idea of 'life', and which was frequently used

One may mention here the 'brazen serpent' which was raised by Moses in the desert,[14] and which is also known to be a symbol of Redemption; in this case the rod on which it was placed is equivalent to the cross and also recalls the 'Tree of Life.'[15] However, the, serpent is most commonly associated with the 'Tree of Knowledge', in which case it is regarded under its maleficent aspect: in fact symbols often have two opposed meanings, as has been shown elsewhere.[16] The serpent that represents life must not be confused with the one representing death, nor the serpent that is a symbol of Christ with the one symbolizing Satan (even when they are so closely combined as they are in the curious figure of the 'amphisbaena' or two-headed serpent). It may be added that the relationship of these two contrary aspects is not without a certain likeness to that of the 'Tree of Life' and the 'Tree of Knowledge'.[17]

We saw just now that a tree of ternary form, such as the 'Sephirothic tree', may in a certain manner synthesize in itself the natures of the 'Tree of Life' and the 'Tree of Knowledge', combining them into a single whole, since the ternary can be split into the unity and the duality of which it is the sum.[18] Instead of one single tree, one sometimes finds three trees joined by their roots, the one in the middle being the 'Tree of Life' and the other two corresponding to the duality of the 'Tree of Knowledge'. Something similar is to be

as a symbol by the Christians of the first two centuries. It is a question whether the first of these two hieroglyphics has not a certain connection with the representation of the 'Tree of Life', and this would link together these two different forms of the cross, since their meaning would thus be partly identical; in any case, there is an obvious connection between the ideas of 'life' and 'health'.

14. Num. 21.

15. The staff of Aesculapius has a similar meaning; in the caduceus of Hermes, we see the two serpents in opposition, corresponding to the double meaning of the symbol.

16. *The King of the World*, chap. 3.

17. A serpent coiled round a tree (or round a staff) is a symbol met with in most traditions; we shall see later what its meaning is from the viewpoint of the geometrical representation of the being and its states.

18. A passage in Honoré d'Urfé's [1567–1625] *Astrea* [Binghamton, NY: Medieval & Renaissance Texts & Studies, 1995] mentions a tree with three shoots, after a tradition which would seem to be of Druidic origin.

found in the depiction of the cross of Christ standing between the two crosses of the good and bad thief: these are set respectively to the right and left of Christ crucified, as the elect and the damned will be at the 'Last Judgment'. While they obviously represent good and evil, in relation to Christ they also correspond to 'Mercy' and 'Rigor', the characteristic attributes of the two lateral columns of the 'Sephirothic tree'. The cross of Christ always occupies the central place which properly belongs to the 'Tree of Life'; and when it is placed between the sun and moon, as it is in most early representations, the same still holds good: it is then truly the 'World Axis'.[19]

In Chinese symbolism, there is a tree with branches joined together at their extremities two by two, which depicts the synthesis of contraries, or the resolution of duality in unity. Sometimes we find a single tree with its branches dividing and rejoining, or there may be two trees having the same root and likewise joined by their branches.[20] They depict the process of universal manifestation: everything starts from unity and returns to unity; in the interim there is duality, the division or differentiation from which manifested existence results; the ideas of unity and duality are thus combined here as in the previous representations.[21] There also exist representations of two distinct trees joined by a single branch (this is known as the 'linked tree'). In this case, a small branch issues from

19. This identification of the cross with the 'World Axis' is explicitly stated in the device of the Carthusians: *Stat Crux dum volvitur orbis*. Cf. the symbol of the 'Globe of the World', in which the cross surmounts the pole and again holds the place of the axis (see *The Esoterism of Dante*, chap. 8).

20. These two forms are met with in particular on *Han* period bas-reliefs.

21. The tree in question bears three-lobed leaves attached to two branches at once, and at the end of its branches are chalice-shaped flowers; birds fly round or perch on the tree. On the connection between the symbolism of birds and that of the tree in different traditions, see *Man and His Becoming*, chap. 3, where various texts from the Upanishads and the Gospel parable of the grain of mustard seed are quoted. A further example, taken from the Scandinavian tradition, is provided by the two crows, Odin's messengers, who alight on the ash *Yggdrasill*, which is one of the forms of the 'World Tree'. In medieval symbolism, birds are again found on the tree *Peridexion*, at the foot of which there is a dragon; the name of this tree is a corruption of *Paradision*, and it may seem rather strange that it should have been thus deformed, as if people had ceased to understand it at a certain moment.

the common branch, which clearly shows that we are concerned with two complementary principles and the product of their union. This product may be taken as representing universal manifestation, the result of the union of 'Heaven' and 'Earth' (the Far-Eastern equivalents of *Purusha* and *Prakriti*), or of the reciprocal action and reaction of *yang* and *yin*, the masculine and feminine elements that all beings proceed from and participate in, and whose combination in perfect equilibrium constitutes (or reconstitutes) the primordial 'Androgyne'.[22]

To return to the representation of the 'Terrestrial Paradise': from its center, that is, from the very foot of the 'Tree of Life', spring four rivers flowing toward the four cardinal points and thus tracing the horizontal cross on the surface of the terrestrial world, that is to say on the plane that corresponds to the domain of the human state. These four rivers, which can be related to the quaternary of the elements[23] and which issue from a single source corresponding to the primordial ether,[24] divide into four parts (corresponding to the four

22. Instead of the 'linked tree', we sometimes also find two rocks joined in the same way; there is in any case a close connection between the tree and the rock (equivalent to the mountain) as symbols of the 'World Axis'; and in a still more general way, there is a constant parallel between the stone and the tree in most traditions.

23. The Kabbalah makes these four rivers correspond to the letters of which the word *PaRDeS* is formed.

24. According to the tradition of the 'Fedeli d'Amore', this source is the 'fountain of youth' (*fons juventutis*), always represented as situated at the foot of a tree; its waters are thus assimilable to the 'draught of immortality' (the *amrita* of the Hindu tradition); the relation of the 'Tree of Life' to the Vedic *Soma* and the Mazdaic *Haoma* are also evident, (cf. *The King of the World*, chaps. 4 and 5). In this connection we should also recall the 'Dew of Light' which, according to the Hebrew Kabbalah, emanates from the 'Tree of Life' and by which the resurrection of the dead is brought about (see ibid., chap. 3); dew likewise plays an important part in Hermetic symbolism. In the Far-Eastern traditions, mention is also made of the 'Tree of Sweet Dew', situated on Mount *Kouen-Lun*, which is often taken as an equivalent of *Meru*, the 'polar' mountain, and the other holy mountains (the mountain, like the tree, being a symbol of the 'World Axis' as already stated). According to the same tradition of the 'Fedeli d'Amore' (see Luigi Valli, *Il Linguaggio segreto di Dante e dei 'Fedeli d'Amore'*), this source is also the 'fount of doctrine', which is connected with the preservation of the primordial tradition at the spiritual center of the world; we thus find here, between the primordial state and the primordial tradition, the link

phases of a cyclic development)[25] the circular precinct of the 'Terrestrial Paradise', which can be regarded as the horizontal section of the spherical form previously referred to as representing the Universe.[26]

The 'Tree of Life' stands at the center of the 'Heavenly Jerusalem', which requires no explanation in view of the relationship of the latter to the 'Terrestrial Paradise':[27] this indicates the reintegration of all things into the primordial state, by virtue of the correspondence between the end of a cycle and its beginning, as will be explained more fully later. It is noteworthy that in the symbolism of the Apocalypse this tree bears twelve fruits,[28] which are assimilable to the twelve *Adityas* of the Hindu tradition.[29] The latter are twelve forms of the sun which will appear simultaneously at the end of the cycle, thus re-entering into the essential unity of their common nature, for they are so many manifestations of one single indivisible essence,

---

indicated elsewhere on the subject of the symbolism of the Holy Grail, regarded under the double aspect of cup and book (*The King of the World*, chap. 5). One may further recall the representation, in Christian symbolism, of the lamb on the book sealed with seven seals, upon the mountain from which the four rivers descend (see ibid., chap. 9); the connection between the symbolism of the 'Tree of Life' and that of the 'Book of Life' will be explained later. Another symbolism which gives rise to interesting parallels is found among certain peoples of Central America, who 'at the intersection of two perpendicular diameters traced in a circle, place the sacred cactus, *peyotl* or *hicouri*, symbolizing the 'cup of immortality', and thus deemed to be situated at the center of a hollow sphere and at the center of the world' (Alexandre Rouhier, *La plante qui fait les yeux emerveilles: Le peyotl* [Paris: G. Doin, 1927], p154). Cf. also, in correspondence with the four rivers, the four sacrificial cups of the *Ribhus* in the *Veda*.

25. See *The Esoterism of Dante*, chap. 8, where, apropos of the 'old man of Crete' who represents the four ages of humanity, we have indicated the existence of an analogical connection between the four rivers of Hades and those of the 'Terrestrial Paradise'.

26. See *The King of the World*, chap. 9.

27. See also ibid., chap. 9. The shape of the 'Heavenly Jerusalem' is not circular but square, final equilibrium having now been attained for the cycle in question [see *The Reign of Quantity*, chaps. 20 and 23. ED.].

28. The fruits of the 'Tree of Life' are the golden apples of the garden of the Hesperides; the 'golden fleece' of the Argonauts, likewise placed on a tree guarded by a serpent or dragon, is another symbol of the immortality which man has to regain.

29. See *The King of the World*, chaps. 4 and 11.

Aditi, which corresponds to the one essence of the 'Tree of Life' itself, whereas *Diti* corresponds to the dual essence of the 'Tree of the Knowledge of good and evil'.[30] Moreover, in various traditions, an image of the sun is often linked with that of a tree, as though the sun were the fruit of the 'World Tree'; it leaves the tree at the beginning of the cycle and comes back to alight on it again at the end.[31] In the Chinese ideograms, the character denoting sunset shows the sun reposing on a tree at the end of the day (analogous to the end of the cycle); darkness is represented by a character depicting the sun fallen at the foot of a tree. In India, we find the triple tree bearing three suns, an image of the *Trimūrti,* as also the tree having as its fruit twelve suns, which, as was just said, are related, like the *Adityas,* to the twelve signs of the zodiac or the twelve months of the year; sometimes there are ten suns, ten being the number of cyclic perfection as in the Pythagorean doctrine.[32] In general, the different suns correspond to the different phases of the cycle; they emerge from unity at the beginning of the cycle and re-enter it at the end, which coincides with the beginning of another cycle by reason of the continuity of all modes of universal Existence.[33]

30. The *Dēvas,* assimilated to the *Adityas,* are said to have issued from *Aditi* (indivisibility); from *Diti* (division) issue the *Daïtyas* or *Asuras. Aditi* is also, in a certain sense, 'primordial nature', called in Arabic *al-fiṭrah.*

31. This is not unconnected with the transfer of the names of certain polar constellations to zodiacal ones and vice versa (*The King of the World,* chap. 10). In a certain sense, the sun may be called the 'son of the Pole'; hence the priority of the 'polar' symbolism over the 'solar'.

32. Cf., in the Hindu doctrine, the ten *Avatāras* that manifest themselves during the course of a *Manvantara.*

33. Among the peoples of Central America, the four ages into which the great cyclic period is divided are regarded as ruled by four different suns, the names of which are drawn from their correspondence with the four elements.

10

THE SWASTIKA

ONE OF THE MOST STRIKING FORMS of the 'horizontal' cross, that is, the cross traced in the plane which represents a certain degree of existence, is the figure of the *swastika*, which indeed seems to be directly attached to the primordial tradition, for it is found in the most diverse and widely separated countries, and from the most remote periods. Far from being an exclusively Eastern symbol as is sometimes thought, it is one of those most generally distributed, from the Far East to the Far West, for it exists even among certain indigenous peoples of America.[1] It is true that at the present day it has been preserved more especially in India and central and eastern Asia, and that perhaps those are the only regions where its meaning is still known, yet even in Europe it has not wholly disappeared.[2] In

1. Quite recently we came across a report which would seem to indicate that the traditions of ancient America are not as completely lost as is supposed, although the writer of the article in which we found it has probably not realized its full import. Here is the passage: 'In 1925, a large part of the Cuna Indians rose, killed the Panama police who were living on their land, and founded the independent republic of *Tulé*, whose flag is a *swastika* on an orange field with a red border. This republic still exists at the present moment' ('Les Indiens de l'Isthme de Panama', by G. Grandidier, *Journal des Debats*, January 22, 1929). Note especially the association of the *swastika* with the name *Tulé* or *Tula*, which is one of the most ancient designations for the supreme spiritual center and is applied also to some of the subordinate centers (see *The King of the World*, chap. 10).

2. In Lithuania and Kurland [a region of Latvia] the peasants still trace this sign on their houses. Doubtless they no longer know its meaning, and see no more in it than a sort of protective talisman; but perhaps the most curious thing is that they give it its Sanskrit name, *swastika*. Lithuanian moreover is the European language most resembling Sanskrit. We completely pass over, needless to say, the artificial and even anti-traditional use of the *swastika* by the German 'racialists', who have given it the fantastic and somewhat ridiculous title of *hakenkreuz* or 'hooked cross',

antiquity this sign occurs among the Celts and in pre-Hellenic Greece;[3] again, in the West, it was anciently one of the emblems of Christ, and it even remained in use as such down to nearly the end of the Middle Ages.[4]

We have said elsewhere that the *swastika* is essentially the 'sign of the Pole'.[5] If it is compared with the figure of the cross inscribed in the circumference of a circle, it will be seen that these are really equivalent symbols in certain respects; but in the *swastika* the rotation round the fixed center, instead of being represented by the circumference, is merely indicated by short lines joined to the ends of the arms of the cross and forming right angles with them; these lines are tangents to the circumference which mark the direction of movement at the corresponding points. Since the circumference

and quite arbitrarily made it a sign of anti-semitism, on the pretext that this emblem must have belonged to the so-called 'Aryan race'. In this connection we would also point out that the name 'gamma cross', which is often given to the *swastika* in the West on account of the resemblance of its branches' shape to that of the Greek letter *gamma*, is equally erroneous; in reality the signs anciently called *gammadia* were quite different, although sometimes in fact found more or less closely associated with the *swastika* in the first centuries of Christianity. One of these signs, also known as the 'cross of the Word' is formed of four *gammas* with their corners pointing inward toward the center; the inner portion of the figure is cruciform, and represents Christ, and the four *gammas* at the corners the four Evangelists; this figure is thus equivalent to the well-known representation of Christ in the middle of the four 'living creatures'. Another arrangement is found in which a central cross is surrounded by four *gammas* placed in square form (with the corners turned outward instead of inward); this figure has the same meaning as the foregoing. Without dwelling further on it, we would add that these signs place the symbolism of the mason's and carpenter's square (whose shape is that of the *gamma*) in direct relationship with that of the cross.

3. There are several variants of the *swastika*, notably one form with curved arms (looking like two intersecting S's), and other forms betraying a relationship with various symbols whose meaning we cannot go into here. The most important of these forms is the one called the 'claviform' *swastika* because its arms are formed of keys; we propose to deal more particularly with this in another study (see *The Great Triad*, chap. 6). Again, certain figures that have retained only a purely decorative character, such as the one known as the 'Greek key pattern', were originally derived from the *swastika*.

4. See *The King of the World*, chap. 1.

5. Ibid., chap. 2. Having there indicated the fantastic interpretations of modern Westerners, we will not return to them here.

represents the manifested world, the fact that it is as it were 'suggested' (or 'understood') indicates quite clearly that the *swastika* is not a symbol of the world, but rather of the Principle's action upon the world.

If we relate the *swastika* to the rotation of a sphere, such as the heavenly sphere, upon its axis, it must be supposed as traced in the equatorial plane, and then the central point, as already explained, will be the projection of the axis on this plane which is perpendicular to it. As for the direction of rotation indicated by the figure, its importance is only secondary and does not affect the general meaning of the symbol; in fact both forms are found, indicating both clockwise and anti-clockwise rotation,[6] and this need not mean that it is always intended to establish an opposition of some kind between them. It is true that in certain countries and epochs schisms from the orthodox tradition may have occurred, and the schismatics, in order to manifest their antagonism, may have deliberately given the figure an orientation contrary to the one used in the environment from which they separated; but this in no way touches the essential meaning, which remains the same in all cases. Besides, the two forms are often found in association, and they can then be regarded as representing one and the same rotation looked at from each of the two poles. This is connected with the very complex symbolism of the two hemispheres, which we cannot go into here.[7]

---

6. In Sanskrit, the word *swastika* is the only one used to denote the symbol in question, in all cases. The term *sauvastika*, which some people have sought to apply to one of the two forms in order to distinguish it from the other (which would then alone be the true *swastika*) is really only an adjective derived from *swastika* and indicating that which relates to that symbol or to its meanings. As for the word *swastika* itself, it is derived from the *su asti*, a form of benediction, which has its exact equivalent in the Hebrew *ki-tōb* of Genesis. Regarding the latter, the fact that it is found repeated at the end of the account of each of the 'days' of the Creation is remarkable enough if one bears this parallel in mind: it seems to indicate that these 'days' are assimilable to so many rotations of the *swastika*, or, in other words, complete revolutions of the 'world wheel', which engender the succession of 'evening and morning' that the text then mentions.

7. In this respect there is a relation between the symbol of the *swastika* and that of the double spiral, likewise most important, and also closely akin to the Far-Eastern *yin-yang* with which we shall be dealing later on.

We cannot think of developing all the considerations to which the symbolism of the *swastika* can give rise, and which in any case are not directly connected with the subject of this study. But its considerable importance from the traditional point of view made it impossible to omit all mention of this special form of the cross.

11

GEOMETRIC
REPRESENTATION
OF THE DEGREES
OF EXISTENCE

IN THE PRECEDING chapters, we have been concerned with examining the various aspects of the symbolism of the cross and showing
their attachment to the metaphysical signification indicated at the
outset. These considerations however are little more than prelimi-
naries, and what must now be developed is the metaphysical signification itself. This involves going as deeply as possible into the
geometrical symbolism which applies equally both to the degrees of
universal Existence and to the states of each being, that is, both
from the 'macrocosmic' and the 'microcosmic' standpoint.

It should first of all be recalled that when the being is considered
in its individual human state, the corporeal individuality is actually
only a restricted portion, a mere mode, of this human individuality.
The integral human individuality is capable of an indefinite development, with modalities of manifestation which are equally indefinite in number, but their sum total still only constitutes one
particular state of the being, wholly situated at one and the same
degree of universal Existence. In the case of the individual human
state, the corporeal modality belongs to the domain of gross or sensible manifestation, and the other modalities to that of subtle manifestation.[1] Each modality is determined by a set of conditions which

---

1. *Man and His Becoming,* chap. 2, and also chaps. 12 and 13. It should also be
noted that when speaking of subtle manifestation, one is often forced to include in

demarcate its possibilities, and each of which, considered apart from the others, may again extend beyond the domain of that modality, and may then combine with different conditions to constitute the domains of other modalities forming part of the same integral individuality.[2] Thus, what determines a certain modality is not exactly a special condition of existence, but rather a combination or association of several conditions. To make this point more completely clear, it would be necessary to take an example such as that of the conditions of corporeal existence, a detailed exposition of which would require, as was said before, a whole study to itself.[3]

Further, when considered from a general standpoint, each of the domains just mentioned contains similar modalities appertaining to an indefinitude of other individuals, each of whom in turn is a state of manifestation of one of the beings in the Universe: here we have states and modalities that correspond to one another in all beings. The sum total of the domains—indefinite in extent—that contain all the modalities of one and the same individuality constitutes one degree of universal Existence, which in its integrality contains an indefinitude of individuals. Naturally, this assumes a degree of Existence corresponding to an individual state, since the human state has been taken as a basis; but all that relates to the manifold modalities holds good equally for any one state, whether individual or non-individual, since the individual condition can introduce restrictive limitations only, though the possibilities it includes do not thereby lose their indefinity.[4]

By virtue of what has been said, a degree of Existence can be represented by a horizontal plane of indefinite extent in two dimensions, which correspond to the two indefinitudes that are to be considered: on the one hand, that of the individuals, which may be

this term the individual non-human states, besides the extra-corporeal modalities of the human state here in question.

2. There are also modalities which are really extensions resulting from the suppression of one or more limiting conditions.

3. On these conditions, see *Man and His Becoming*, chap. 24.

4. As has already been stated, an individual state is one that includes form among its determining conditions, so that 'individual manifestation' and 'formal manifestation' are equivalent expressions.

represented by the sum of the straight lines in the plane that are parallel to one of the dimensions, which, if desired, may be defined by the intersection of this horizontal plane with a frontal plane;[5] and on the other hand that of the domains peculiar to the individuals' different modalities, which will then be represented by the sum of the straight lines in the horizontal plane that are perpendicular to the foregoing direction, that is, the ones parallel to the visual or fore-and-aft axis, the direction of which defines the other dimension.[6] Each of these two classes includes an indefinitude of parallel straight lines, all indefinite in length; each point in the plane will be determined by the intersection of two straight lines, one from each class, and hence will represent a particular modality of one of the individuals comprised in the degree considered.

Each of the degrees of universal Existence (which embraces an indefinitude of them) may be similarly represented, in a three-dimensional space, by a horizontal plane. It has just been shown that a section of such a plane by a frontal plane represents an individual—or rather, speaking in a more general way and one capable of being applied without distinction to all degrees, represents a certain state of a being, a state which may be individual or non-individual, according to the conditions of the degree of Existence it belongs to. Thus a frontal plane may now be regarded as representing a being in its totality. This being comprises an indefinite

5. If these terms borrowed from perspective are to be rightly understood, it must be recalled that a frontal plane is a particular case of a vertical plane, whereas a horizontal plane, on the contrary, is a particular case of an endview plane. Conversely, a vertical straight line is a particular case of a plane projection, and a vertical projection is a particular case of a horizontal straight line. It must also be observed that through every point there passes one single vertical line and an indefinite multitude of horizontal lines, but only one horizontal plane (containing all the horizontal lines that pass through that point) and an indefinite multitude of vertical planes (all passing through the vertical straight line, which is their common intersection, and each being determined by that vertical line and one of the horizontal lines passing through the point in question).

6. In the horizontal plane, the direction of the first dimension is that of the plane projections (or transversal straight lines), and the direction of the second is that of the vertical projections.

multiplicity of states, which are then depicted by all the horizontal lines in that plane; on the other hand, the vertical lines in the plane are formed by the groups of modalities that respectively correspond to one another in all these states. Furthermore, in three-dimensional space there is an indefinitude of such planes, representing the indefinitude of the beings contained in the entire Universe.

12

GEOMETRIC
REPRESENTATION
OF THE STATES
OF THE BEING

IN THE THREE-DIMENSIONAL REPRESENTATION just given, each modality of any state of the being is indicated by a point alone; however, such a modality is itself also capable of developing in the course of a cycle of manifestation involving an indefinitude of secondary modifications. Thus, in the corporeal modality of the human individuality, for example, these modifications will be all the moments of its existence (regarded, naturally, under the aspect of temporal succession, which is one of the conditions to which this modality is subjected), or, which amounts to the same thing, all the acts and motions whatsoever that it will perform in the course of this existence.[1] If all these modifications are to be included in our representation, then the modality considered will have to be depicted, not merely by a point, but by a whole straight line, each point in which will now be one of the secondary modifications in question; and here it should be carefully noted that this straight line, although indefinite, is nonetheless limited; in fact, everything indefinite is limited, and so is (if the expression is permissible) every

---

1. We purposely here use the word 'motions', because it alludes to a metaphysical theory which is most important but does not fall within the scope of the present study. A summary notion of this theory can be obtained by referring to what we have said elsewhere on the subject of the idea of *apurva* in the Hindu doctrine and of 'concordant actions and reactions' (*Introduction to the Study of Hindu Doctrines*, pt. 2, chap. 13).

power of the indefinite.[2] Simple indefinitude being represented by a straight line, double indefinitude or the indefinite to the power of two will be represented by a plane, and triple indefinitude or the indefinite to the power of three by a three-dimensional expanse. If therefore each modality, envisaged as a simple indefinitude, is depicted by a straight line, a state of the being, involving an indefinitude of such modalities—in other words a double indefinitude—will be depicted in its entirety by a horizontal plane, and a being in its totality, with the indefinitude of its states, will be represented by a three-dimensional expanse. This new representation is thus more complete than the former one, but it is clear that unless three-dimensional space is departed from, we can here consider only a single being, and not, as previously, the whole of the beings in the Universe, for the consideration of the totality of beings would make it necessary to introduce a further indefinitude, which would be of the fourth order, and could not be geometrically depicted except by imagining a fourth dimension superadded to space.[3]

In this new representation, we see first of all that through each point in the extension under consideration there pass three straight lines, respectively parallel to the three dimensions of this extension; each point can therefore be taken as the apex of a trihedral right-angle, constituting a system of coordinates to which the whole extension may be referred, and the three axes of which will form the three-dimensional cross. If the vertical axis of this system be taken as given, it will meet each horizontal plane in a point, which will be the origin of the rectangular coordinates to which that plane will be

2. The indefinite, which proceeds from the finite, is always reducible thereto, since it is only the development of the possibilities included or implied in the finite. It is an elementary truth, though one too often overlooked, that the alleged 'mathematical infinite' (a quantitative indefinitude either numerical or geometrical) is not infinite at all, for it is limited by the determination inherent in its own nature. [See also *The Metaphysical Principles of the Infinitesimal Calculus*, passim, but especially chaps. 1, 2, 7, and 8. ED.]

3. This is not the place to deal with the question of the 'fourth dimension' of space, which has given rise to many erroneous or fantastic notions, and which would find a more natural place in a study of the conditions of corporeal existence. [See *The Reign of Quantity*, chap. 18, where these errors are examined. ED.]

referred, and the two axes of which will form a two-dimensional cross. It can be said that this point is the center of the plane, and the vertical axis is the locus of the centers of all the horizontal planes; every vertical, in other words every line parallel to this axis, also contains points which correspond to one another in those planes. If, in addition to the vertical axis, a particular horizontal plane is taken as the basis of the system of coordinates, then the trihedral right-angle just mentioned will also be wholly determined thereby. There will be a two-dimensional cross, traced by two of the three axes, in each of the three planes of coordinates, one of which is the horizontal plane in question, while the others are the two orthogonal planes each passing through the vertical axis and through one of the horizontal axes; and these three crosses will have as their common center the apex of the trihedral angle, which is the center of the three-dimensional cross and may thus be also regarded as the center of the whole extension. Every point could be the center, and, one may say, potentially is so; but in fact it is necessary for one particular point to be given in order to be actually able to draw the cross, in other words to measure the whole extension, or, analogically, to realize the total scope of the being's possibilities.

13

RELATIONSHIP BETWEEN THE TWO FOREGOING REPRESENTATIONS

IN THE SECOND THREE-DIMENSIONAL representation, in which only one being in its totality was considered, both the horizontal direction in which the modalities of all the states of this being develop and the vertical planes that are parallel to it, imply an idea of logical succession, whereas the vertical planes that are perpendicular to it correspond, correlatively, to the idea of logical simultaneity.[1] If we project the whole expanse on to the plane of coordinates which corresponds to the idea of simultaneity, then each modality of each state of the being will be projected on a point of a horizontal straight line, this line itself being the projection of the entirety of a certain state of the being; and in particular, the state whose center coincides with that of the total being will be depicted by the horizontal axis lying in the plane on to which the projection is made. We thus come back to our first representation, that in which the being is situated wholly in a vertical plane; a horizontal plane can then once again represent a degree of universal Existence, and the establishment of this correspondence between the two representations, by allowing us to pass readily from the one to the other, will enable us to avoid departing from three-dimensional space.

Each horizontal plane, when it represents a degree of universal Existence, comprehends the whole development of a particular

1. Naturally the ideas of succession and simultaneity must here be conceived from the purely logical viewpoint only, and not the chronological, because time is merely a special condition, not indeed of the human state as a whole, but of certain modalities of it.

possibility, the manifestation of which, as a whole, constitutes what may be called a 'macrocosm', that is, a world, whereas in the other representation, which relates to a single being alone, the plane is only the development of the same possibility in that being, constituting one of the being's states, whether individual or non-individual, which may be called by analogy a 'microcosm'. Further, it is most important to observe that when considered in isolation the 'macrocosm' itself, like the 'microcosm', is only one of the elements of the Universe, just as each particular possibility is only one element of total Possibility.

Of the two representations, the one that relates to the Universe may, for simplicity of language, be called the 'macrocosmic' representation, and the one that relates to a being, the 'microcosmic'. We have seen how the three-dimensional cross is traced in the latter; the same will hold good in the 'macrocosmic' representation if the corresponding elements in it are determined—namely a vertical axis, which will be the axis of the Universe, and a horizontal plane, which by analogy may be termed its equator. And it must also be pointed out that each 'macrocosm' has here its center on the vertical axis, as did each 'microcosm' in the other representation.

The above shows the analogy that exists between the 'macrocosm' and the 'microcosm', every part of the Universe being analogous to the other parts, and its own parts also being analogous to it, because all are analogous to the total Universe. It follows that if we consider the 'macrocosm', each of the definite domains that it comprises is analogous to it; similarly, if we consider the 'microcosm', each of its modalities is also analogous to it. Thus, to take a particular instance, the corporeal modality of the human individuality can be taken as symbolizing, in its various parts, that same individuality envisaged as a whole.[2] It must be remembered however that the individuality embraces an indefinite multitude of co-existing modalities, just as the bodily organism itself is composed of an indefinite multitude of cells, each of which also has an existence of its own.

2. See *Man and His Becoming*, chap. 12.

14

THE SYMBOLISM
OF WEAVING

THERE IS A SYMBOLISM which is directly related to what has gone before, although it is sometimes applied in a way that may at first sight seem a little remote from our subject. In Eastern doctrines, traditional books are frequently referred to by terms which in their literal sense are connected with weaving. Thus, in Sanskrit, *sūtra* properly means 'thread'[1]: a book may be formed by a collection of *sūtras*, as a fabric is formed by a tissue of threads; *tantra* also has the meaning of 'thread' and that of 'fabric', and denotes more particularly the 'warp' of a fabric.[2] Similarly in Chinese *king* is the 'warp' of a material, and *wei* is its 'weft'; the first of these two words denotes at the same time a fundamental book, and the second denotes the commentaries on it.[3] This distinction between the 'warp' and the

1. This word is identical with the Latin *sutura*, the same root, with the meaning of 'to sew', being found in both languages. It is at least curious to note that the Arabic word *sūrat*, which denotes chapters of the Koran, is composed of exactly the same elements as the Sanskrit *sūtra*; this word has in addition the kindred sense of 'row' or 'line', and its derivation is unknown.

2. The root *tan* of this word expresses in the first place the idea of extension.

3. The use of knotted cords, which took the place of writing in China at a very distant period, is also attached to the weaving symbolism; these cords were of the same kind as those used by the ancient Peruvians and called by them *quipos*. Though it has sometimes been maintained that these were merely for counting, it seems clear that they also expressed far more complex ideas, especially since we are told that they formed the 'annals of the empire', and since the Peruvians never had any other mode of writing, whereas they possessed a highly perfected and refined language. This kind of ideography was made possible by multiple combinations in which the use of threads of different colors played an important part.

'weft', in the corpus of traditional scriptures, corresponds to the distinction drawn in Hindu terminology between *Shruti*, which is the fruit of direct inspiration, and *Smriti*, which is the product of reflection upon the contents of *Shruti*.[4]

If the meaning of this symbolism is to be clearly grasped, it should first be observed that the warp, formed as it is by threads stretched upon the loom, represents the immutable, principial elements, whereas the threads of the weft, which pass between those of the warp by the to-and-fro movement of the shuttle, represent the variable and contingent elements, in other words the applications of the principle to this or that set of particular conditions. Again, if one thread of the warp and one of the weft are considered, it will at once be seen that their meeting forms the cross, of which they are respectively the vertical line and the horizontal; and every stitch in the fabric, being thus the meeting-point of two mutually perpendicular threads, is thereby the center of such a cross. Now, following what was said about the general symbolism of the cross, the vertical line represents that which joins together all the degrees of Existence by connecting their corresponding points to one another, whereas the horizontal line represents the development of one of these states or degrees. Thus the horizontal direction may be taken as depicting, for example, the human state, and the vertical direction that which is transcendent in relation to that state. This transcendence clearly belongs to *Shruti*, which is essentially 'non-human', whereas *Smriti* involves applications to the human order and is produced by the exercise of the specifically human faculties.

At this point another observation may be made which will bring out still more clearly the concordance of different symbolisms which are more closely connected than might be supposed; this concerns the aspect of the cross in which it symbolizes the union of complements. In this aspect, as we have seen, the vertical line represents the active or masculine principle (*Purusha*), and the horizontal one the passive or feminine principle (*Prakriti*), all manifestation

---

4. See *Man and His Becoming*, chap. 1 and also *Spiritual Authority and Temporal Power*, chap. 8.

being produced by the 'actionless' influence of the first upon the second. Now, in another context, *Shruti* is likened to direct light, depicted by the sun, and *Smriti* to reflected[5] light, depicted by the moon; but, at the same time, the sun and moon, in nearly all traditions, also respectively symbolize the masculine and feminine principles in universal manifestation.

The weaving symbolism is not applied merely to traditional scriptures; it is also used to represent the world, or more precisely the aggregate of all the worlds, that is, the indefinite multitude of the states or degrees that constitute universal Existence. Thus, in the Upanishads, the supreme *Brahma* is called 'That upon which the worlds are woven, as warp and weft,' or by other similar formulas;[6] here again, warp and weft naturally have the respective meanings just defined. Again, according to the Taoist doctrine, all beings are subject to the continual alternation of the two states of life and death (condensation and dissipation, vicissitudes of *yang* and *yin*);[7] and the commentators call this alternation 'the to-and-fro motion of the shuttle upon the cosmic loom.'[8] Actually, these two applications of one and the same symbolism are even more closely akin, since in certain traditions the Universe itself is sometimes symbolized by a book; in this connection, one need only recall the *Liber*

---

5. The double meaning of the word 'reflection' is worthy of note.

6. *Mundaka Upanishad* ii.2.5; *Brihad-Āranyaka Upanishad* iii.8.7–8. The Buddhist monk Kumarajīva translated into Chinese a Sanskrit work entitled *The Net of Brahma (Fan-wang-king)*, according to which the worlds are arranged like the meshes of a net.

7. *Tao Te Ching*, chap. 16.

8. Chang-Hung Yang also compares this alternation to breathing, the active inspiration corresponding to life and the passive expiration to death, the end of the one being moreover the beginning of the other. The same commentator also makes use of the lunar rotation as a term of comparison, the full moon signifying life and the new moon death, with two intermediate periods of waxing and waning. As regards breathing, what is said here refers to the two phases of existence of a being as if he himself were the breather; in the universal order, on the other hand, out-breathing corresponds to the development of manifestation, and inbreathing to the return to the non-manifested, as was said earlier; according as things are considered in respect of manifestation or in respect of the Principle, one must not forget to apply the 'inverse sense' in analogy.

Mundi of the Brotherhood of the Rose-Cross, and also the well-known Apocalyptic symbol of the *Liber Vitae*.[9] From this standpoint again, the threads of the warp, by which the corresponding points in all states are connected, form the sacred book which is the prototype (or rather, archetype) of all traditional scriptures, and of which these scriptures are merely expressions in human language.[10] The threads of the weft, each of which is the development of events in a certain state, form the commentary, in the sense that they give the applications relating to the different states; all events, envisaged in the simultaneity of the 'timeless', are thus inscribed in the Book, of which each represents as it were one character, being also identified with one stitch in the fabric. On this symbolism of the book, the following passage from Muḥyi 'd-Dīn ibn al-'Arabī may also be quoted: 'The Universe is a vast book; the characters of this book are all written, in principle, with the same ink and transcribed on to the eternal Tablet by the Divine Pen; all are transcribed simultaneously and inseparably; for that reason the essential phenomena hidden in the 'secret of secrets' were given the name of 'transcendent letters'. And these same transcendent letters, that is to say all creatures, after having being virtually condensed in the Divine Omniscience, were carried down on the Divine Breath to the lower lines, and composed and formed the manifested Universe.'[11]

Another form of the symbolism of weaving, also found in the Hindu tradition, is the image of the spider weaving its web; this image is even more exact, since the spider spins the thread out of its own substance.[12] By reason of the web's circular shape, which may

9. As was stated earlier, in certain representations the book sealed with seven seals, with the lamb lying upon it, is placed, like the 'Tree of Life', at the common source of the four rivers of Paradise. We also remarked upon the relationship between the symbolism of the tree and that of the book: the leaves of the tree and the characters in the book alike represent all the beings in the Universe (the 'ten thousand beings' of the Far-Eastern tradition).

10. This is expressly affirmed of the Veda and the Koran; the idea of the 'Eternal Gospel' also shows that this same conception is not wholly foreign to Christianity.

11. *Al-Futūḥāt al-Mekkiyah*. One might compare the part likewise played by letters in the cosmogonic doctrine of the *Sepher Yetsirah*.

12. Commentary of Shankarāchārya on the *Brahma-Sūtras* II.1.25.

be considered as the plane section of the cosmogonic spheroid, that is, of the non-closed sphere alluded to earlier on, the warp is here represented by the threads radiating from the center, and the weft by the threads arranged in concentric circles.[13] To return from this to the ordinary representation of weaving, it is only necessary to consider the center as being indefinitely remote, so that the radii become parallel in the vertical direction, while the concentric circles become straight lines perpendicular to these radii, that is, horizontal lines.

To sum up, the warp may be said to represent the principles that bind together all the worlds or all the states, each of its threads forming the connection between corresponding points in these different states, whereas the weft represents the chains of events that are produced in each of the worlds, each thread being thus the development of events in a given world. From another point of view it may be said that the manifestation of a being in a certain state of existence, like any other event, is determined by the meeting of a thread of the warp with a thread of the weft. Each thread of the warp is then a being envisaged in its essential nature, which insofar as it is a direct projection of the principial 'Self' provides the connecting-link between all its states, and maintains its unity through their indefinite multiplicity. In this case, the thread of the weft which this thread of the warp meets at a given point corresponds to a definite state of existence, and the intersection of the two threads determines the relation of the being, as regards its manifestation in that state, with the cosmic environment in which it is thus situated. The individual nature of a human being, for instance, is the resultant of the meeting of these two threads; in other words, it will always be necessary to distinguish in him two kinds of elements which will have to be referred to the vertical and the horizontal directions respectively: the first are the elements that properly belong to the being in question, whereas the second proceed from the environmental conditions.

13. The spider, at the center of its web, corresponds to the sun surrounded by its rays; it can thus be taken as a figure of the 'Heart of the World'.

By a different but equivalent symbolism, the threads of which the 'world fabric' is formed are also termed the 'hair of *Shiva*';[14] they might be metaphorically described as the 'lines of force' of the manifested Universe, and the directions of space represent them in the corporeal order. It will readily be seen in how many different ways all these considerations are capable of being applied; but the sole purpose of this chapter was to indicate the essential meaning of the symbolism of weaving, which apparently is very little known in the West.[15]

14. See above, on the subject of the directions of space.

15. Nevertheless, traces of a symbolism of the same kind are to be found in Greco-Roman antiquity, notably in the myth of the Fates; but this really seems to relate rather to the threads of the weft alone, and its 'fateful' character may in fact be explained by the absence of the notion of the warp, that is, by the fact that the being is envisaged solely in its individual state, without any conscious intervention (for that being) of its transcendent personal principle. This interpretation is further justified by the way in which Plato regards the vertical axis in the myth of Er the Armenian (*Republic*, Book X): according to him, in fact, the luminous axis of the world is the 'spindle of Necessity'; it is an axis of diamond, surrounded by a number of concentric sheaths, of different dimensions and colors, which correspond to the different planetary spheres; the Fate Clotho makes it turn with her right hand, hence from right to left, which is also the most usual and normal direction of rotation of the *swastika*. Apropos of this 'diamond axis', the Tibetan symbol of the *vajra*, a name which means both 'thunderbolt' and 'diamond', is also related to the 'World Axis'.

15

REPRESENTATION
OF THE CONTINUITY OF
THE MODALITIES OF ONE
AND THE SAME STATE
OF THE BEING

If we consider one of the being's states, depicted by a horizontal plane in the 'microcosmic' representation that we have described, it remains to say more precisely what the center of this plane and also the vertical axis that passes through this center correspond to. But, to reach that point, it will be necessary to introduce a further geometrical representation, which will show not only, as hitherto, the parallelism or correspondence, but also the continuity that exists between the modalities of each state as well as between the different states themselves.

For this purpose, the figure will have to undergo a change, which corresponds to what in analytical geometry is termed a passage from a system of rectilinear coordinates to a system of polar coordinates. Instead of representing different modalities of one and the same state by parallel straight lines, as previously, we can represent them by concentric circumferences described in the same horizontal plane, and having their common center at the center of the plane itself, that is to say, at its meeting-point with the vertical axis.

In this way, it becomes evident that each modality is finite and limited, because it is represented by a circumference, which is a closed curve, or at least a line whose ends are known and as it were given.[1] On the other hand this circumference contains an indefinite multitude of points,[2] representing the indefinitude of secondary modifications that are comprised in the modality considered, whatever it may be.[3] Further, the concentric circumferences must leave no interval between one another, apart from the infinitesimal distance between two immediately adjacent points (we shall return to this question a little later), so that the totality of these circumferences will comprise all the points in the plane, which implies that there is continuity between them. However, to achieve a real continuity, the end of each circumference must coincide with the beginning of the following one (and not that of the same circumference); and for this to be possible without the two successive circumferences being confounded, it is necessary that these circumferences,

1. The reservation is necessary in order that this may not seem to contradict what is to follow.

2. It is important to notice that we do not say an indefinite number, but indefinite multitude, because it is possible that the indefinitude in question may exceed all number, even though the series of numbers is itself indefinite, but in discontinuous mode, whereas that of the points in a line is so in continuous mode. The term 'multitude' is broader and more comprehensive than that of 'numerical multiplicity', and can even apply outside the domain of quantity, of which number is only a special mode; this was clearly realized by the scholastic philosophers, who transposed this notion of 'multitude' into the order of 'transcendentals', that is, universal modes of Being, where it stands in the same analogical relation to that of numerical multiplicity as the conception of metaphysical Unity stands to that of arithmetical or quantitative unity. It is, of course, this 'transcendental' multiplicity that is in question when we speak of the multiple states of the being, for quantity is only a particular condition applicable to certain of those states.

3. As the length of a circumference increases the further the circumference is from the center, one might at first suppose that it contains more points; yet if we reflect that every point in a circumference is the end of one of its radii, it follows that there are no more points in the greater circumference than in the lesser. Besides, if there are always as many points (if it is possible to employ such a mode of speech under these conditions) in a circumference that diminishes as it approaches its center, then as this circumference is in the limiting case reduced to the center itself, the center, though being only a single point, must contain all the points in the circumference; which amounts to saying that all things are contained in unity.

or rather the curves that we have been regarding as such, shall be in actual fact non-closed curves.

Indeed, we can go further in this direction: it is physically impossible in fact to describe a line that is truly a closed curve. To prove this, it is sufficient to observe that, in the space in which our corporeal modality is situated, everything is ceaselessly in motion (owing to the effect of the spatial and temporal conditions, of which motion is as it were a resultant); so that, if we want to describe a circumference, and start at a given point in space, we shall necessarily find ourselves at a different point when we have completed it, and shall never again pass through the starting-point. Similarly, the curve that symbolizes the course of any evolutive cycle[4] will never have to pass twice through one and the same point, which is tantamount to saying that there cannot be a closed curve (nor a curve containing 'multiple points'). This representation illustrates that there cannot be two identical possibilities in the Universe, which indeed would amount to a limitation of total Possibility—an impossible limitation, because, since it would have to contain Possibility, it could not be contained therein. Thus any limitation of universal Possibility is in the strict and proper sense of the word an impossibility; and for this reason all philosophical systems, which, qua systems, explicitly or implicitly postulate such limitations, stand equally condemned from a metaphysical standpoint.[5] To return to identical or supposedly identical possibilities, it should also be pointed out, for greater exactitude, that two possibilities that were truly identical would not differ in respect of any of their

---

4. By 'evolutive cycle' we merely mean—following the original sense of the word—the process of development of the possibilities contained in any one mode of existence, without its being implied that this process can have the slightest relation to any 'evolutionist' theory (cf. *Man and His Becoming*, chap. 17); we have so often expressed our views about such theories that the point need not be labored here.

5. It will be seen, moreover, that this excludes all the more or less 'reincarnationist' theories that have sprung up in the modem West, on the same grounds as Nietzsche's famous 'eternal recurrence' and other similar conceptions; these considerations are set forth in detail in *The Spiritist Fallacy*, pt. 2, chap. 6.

conditions of realization; but if all the conditions are the same, then it is also the same possibility and not two distinct ones, since there is then coincidence in all respects.[6] This reasoning can be strictly applied to all the points in our representation, each of these points depicting a particular modification which realizes a certain given possibility.[7]

The beginning and the end of any one of the circumferences we have to consider, then, are not the same point, but two consecutive points on one and the same radius, and in reality they cannot even be said to belong to the same circumference: one still belongs to the preceding one, of which it is the end, and the other to the following one, of which it is the beginning. The extreme terms of an indefinite series can be regarded as situated outside that series, by the very fact that they establish its continuity with other series; and all this can be applied, in particular, to the birth and death of the corporeal modality of the human individuality. Thus, the two extreme modifications of each modality do not coincide, but there is simply correspondence between them in the state of the being of which those modalities form part, this correspondence being indicated by the situation of the points representing them on one and the same radius from the center of the plane. Consequently, the same radius will contain the extreme modifications of all the modalities of the state in question, but the modalities should not be regarded, properly speaking, as successive (for they can just as well be simultaneous), but only as logically linked together. The curves that depict these modalities, instead of being circumferences as we had originally supposed, are the successive turns of an indefinite spiral described in the horizontal plane and developing outward from its center. This curve continuously broadens out, the radius varying by

6. This is a point which Leibnitz seems to have seen well enough when enunciating his 'principle of indiscernibles', though he has perhaps not framed it so clearly (cf. *Spiritual Authority and Temporal Power*, chap. 7).

7. The term 'possibility' is here taken in its most restricted and specialized sense: what is in question is not even one particular possibility capable of an indefinite development, but only any one of the elements that such a development involves.

an infinitesimal quantity, namely the distance between two consecutive points on the radius. The distance may be deemed as small as one likes, in accordance with the actual definition of infinitesimal quantities, namely quantities capable of diminishing indefinitely; but it can never be regarded as nil, for the two consecutive points are not confounded; were it able to become nil, then there would no longer be anything but one and the same point.

16

RELATIONSHIP
BETWEEN THE
POINT AND SPACE

THE QUESTION RAISED BY THE FINAL OBSERVATION in the last chapter calls for further examination, but we do not propose to go fully into the question of space in all its implications, since this would more properly fall within the compass of a study of the conditions of corporeal existence. The first thing to be said is that the distance between two immediately adjacent points, which we have been led to consider as a result of the introduction of continuity into the geometrical representation of the being, may be regarded as the limit of space in the sense of indefinitely decreasing quantities; in other words, it is the smallest space possible, after which there remains no spatial condition at all, and it would not be possible to suppress it without departing from the realm of existence that is subject to that condition. Therefore, when space is divided indefinitely,[1] and when this division is carried as far as is possible, that is, to the limits of the spatial possibility by which divisibility is conditioned (and which is indefinite in the decreasing as well as the increasing sense), what is arrived at as the final result is not a point, but rather the elementary distance between two points. It follows

---

1. We say 'indefinitely', but not 'to infinity', which would be an absurdity, divisibility being necessarily an attribute proper to a limited domain, because the spatial condition, on which it depends, is itself essentially limited; hence there must be a limit to divisibility, as there is to any relativity or determination whatsoever; and we can be certain that this limit exists, even though it is not at present accessible to us.

from this that for spatial extension to exist there must be already two points, and the (one-dimensional) expanse which is realized by their simultaneous presence, and which is precisely the distance between them constitutes a third element which expresses the relationship between the two points, by at once joining and separating them. This distance, moreover, when regarded as a relation, is plainly not composed of parts, for if it were, the parts into which it could be resolved would simply be other relationships of distance, of which it is logically independent, just as from the numerical point of view unity is independent of fractions.[2] This is true for any distance, when envisaged solely in respect of the two points that are its extremities, and is *a fortiori* true for an infinitesimal distance, which is in no way a definite quantity at all, but solely expresses a spatial relation between two immediately adjacent points, such as two consecutive points in any line. Again, the points themselves, considered as extremities of a distance, are not parts of the spatial continuum, although the distance-relation assumes that they are conceived as situated in space; it is thus really distance that is the true spatial element.

Thus it is not possible in all strictness to say that a line is formed of points, and the reason for this is not difficult to understand, for, since each of the points is without extension, their mere addition, even if they are of an indefinite multitude, can never form an extension; in reality, the line is constituted by the elementary distances between its consecutive points. In the same way, and for a similar reason, if we consider an indefinitude of parallel straight lines in a plane, we cannot say that the plane is constituted by the combination of all these lines, or that they are true constitutive elements of the plane; the true elements are the distances between those lines, distances which make them distinct lines and not confounded, and

2. Properly speaking, fractions cannot be 'parts of unity', for true unity is obviously without parts; this faulty definition of fractions implies a confusion between numerical unity, which is essentially indivisible, and 'units of measurement', which are unities in only a quite relative and conventional manner, and which, being of the nature of continuous magnitudes, are necessarily divisible and composed of parts. [For all the foregoing reasoning, see also *The Metaphysical Principles of the Infinitesimal Calculus*, especially chap. 8. ED.]

if the lines do form the plane in a certain sense, it is not by themselves but by their distances that they do so, as in the case of the
points of a line. Again, a three-dimensional extension is not composed of an indefinitude of parallel planes, but of the distances
between all those planes.

However, the primordial element, that which exists by itself, is
the point, since it is presupposed by distance and distance is only a
relationship; hence space itself presupposes the point. The latter
may be said to contain in itself a virtuality of extension, which it can
only develop by first duplicating itself, placing itself so to speak
opposite to itself, and then by multiplying (or better, sub-multiply-
ing) itself indefinitely, so that manifested space in its entirety proceeds from differentiation of the point, or, to speak more exactly,
from the point insofar as it differentiates itself. This differentiation
however is real only from the point of view of spatial manifestation;
it is illusory in respect of the principial point itself, which does not
thereby cease to be in itself that which it was, and whose essential
unity can in no way be affected thereby.[3] The point, considered in
itself, is in no wise subject to the spatial condition, for on the contrary it is the principle of that condition: it is the point that realizes
space and produces extension by its act, which, in the temporal condition (but only therein), is translated by movement; but, in order
to realize space thus, it is bound, by some one of its modalities, to
situate itself in space, which indeed is nothing without it, and which
it will completely fill by the deployment of its own virtualities.[4] Successively in the temporal condition, or simultaneously outside that

3. If spatial manifestation disappears, all the points situated in space are
resorbed into the single principial point, since there is no longer any distance
between them.

4. Leibnitz has rightly distinguished between what he calls 'metaphysical
points', which for him are the true 'units of substance', and which are independent
of space, and 'mathematical points', which are only simple modalities of the former,
inasmuch as they are their spatial determinations, constituting their respective
'points of view' in order to represent or express the Universe. For Leibnitz also it is
what is situated in space that makes the whole reality of space itself; but it is evident
that one cannot, as he does, relate to space everything that constitutes, in each
being, the expression of the entire Universe.

condition (which, be it observed in passing, would take us outside ordinary three-dimensional space),[5] it identifies itself with all the potential points in space in order to realize the latter. Thus space must be regarded as no more than a mere potentiality of being, which is nothing else than the total virtuality of the point conceived in its passive aspect, the locus or container of all the manifestations of its activity, a container that has no existence except through the realization of its possible content.[6]

Being without dimensions, the primordial point is also without form; hence it does not belong to the order of individual existences. It does not individualize itself in any way except when it situates itself in space, and then not in itself, but solely by one of its modalities, so that strictly speaking it is these latter that are really individualized, and not the principial point. Moreover, if there is to be form, there must already be differentiation, hence multiplicity realized in a certain measure, which is possible only when the point opposes itself, if the expression is permissible, by means of two or more of its modalities of spatial manifestation; and it is this opposition, fundamentally, that constitutes distance. The realization of distance is the first accomplishment of space, which without it, as we have said, is but a mere potentiality of receptiveness. We would also observe that distance at first exists only virtually in the spherical form that was mentioned earlier, which is the form that corresponds to the minimum of differentiation, being 'isotropic' in respect of the central point, with nothing to distinguish one particular direction from any other; the radius, which is here the expression of distance (taken from the center to the periphery), is not actually drawn and does not form a component part of the spherical figure. The actual realization of distance is made explicit only in the straight line, of

5. The transmutation of succession into simultaneity in the integration of the human state implies a sort of 'spatialization' of time that may be translated by the addition of a fourth dimension.

6. It will be seen that the relation of the principial point to virtual (or rather potential) extension is analogous to that of 'essence' to 'substance', these two terms being taken in their universal sense, that is, as denoting the two poles of manifestation, active and passive, which the Hindu doctrine calls *Purusha* and *Prakriti* (see *Man and His Becoming*, chap. 4).

which it is the initial and fundamental element, as the result of the specifying of a certain given direction. Thereafter, space can no longer be regarded as 'isotropic'; from this standpoint it must be referred to two symmetrical poles (the two points between which there is distance) instead of being referred to a single center.

The point, which realizes the whole of space, as has just been shown, makes itself the center of space by measuring it along all its dimensions through the indefinite extension of the branches of the cross in the six directions, or toward the six cardinal points of space. It is thus 'Universal Man', of whom this cross is the symbol (and not individual man, who, as such, can realize nothing outside his own state of being), that is truly the 'measure of all things', to use the expression of Protagoras which we have quoted elsewhere,[7] though it is unlikely that the Greek sophist was himself aware of this metaphysical interpretation.[8]

7. *Man and His Becoming*, chap. 16.

8. Had it been our present intention to undertake a more complete study of the spatial condition and its limitations, we might have shown how a proof of the absurdity of atomistic theories can be deduced from the considerations set forth in this chapter. Without dwelling further on the point, it may be observed that everything corporeal is necessarily divisible, by the very fact of being extended, that is, subject to the spatial condition. (Cf. *Introduction to the Study of the Hindu Doctrines*, pt. 2, chap. 10).

17

ONTOLOGY OF
THE BURNING BUSH

THE SIGNIFICANCE OF THE DOUBLING of the point by polarization will be even clearer if we look at it from a strictly ontological
point of view; but first of all let us consider it from a logical or even
merely grammatical standpoint. Here, in fact, there are three elements, namely the two points and the distance between them, and it
will be seen that these three elements correspond exactly to those of
a proposition: the two points represent its two terms, while their
distance from each other, expressing the relation between them,
plays the part of the 'copula', that is, the element that connects the
two terms. If the proposition is considered in its commonest and
most general form, namely the attributive proposition, in which the
'copula' is the verb 'to be',[1] it will be seen that it expresses an identity,
at least in a certain respect, between the subject and the attribute;
the reason is that the two points are really only the duplication of
one and the same point, which has so to speak taken up a position
confronting itself, as has been explained.

The relation between the two terms can also be conceived as a
relation of knowledge. In this case, the being, confronting itself as it
were in order to know itself, duplicates itself into subject and object;
but here again the two are one in reality. This may be extended to all
true knowledge, essentially implying as it does an identification of
subject and object, which can be expressed by saying that in the

---

1. All the other forms of propositions considered by logicians can always be
reduced to the attributive form, because the relationship expressed by the latter has
a more essential and fundamental character than any other.

relation and the measure in which there is knowledge, the knower is the known. It now becomes clear that this point of view is directly connected with the former one, for it can be said that the known object is an attribute (that is, a modality) of the knower-subject.

If we now consider universal Being, which is represented by the principial point in its indivisible unity, and of which all beings insofar as they are manifested in Existence are really no more than 'participations', it can be said to polarize into subject and attribute without having its unity affected thereby. The proposition of which it is at once subject and attribute then takes the form: 'Being is Being'. This is the actual enunciation of what logicians call the 'principle of identity'; but, in this form, its real scope clearly transcends the domain of logic, and is properly and primarily an ontological proposition, whatever applications in different orders may be extracted from it. It may also be said to express the relation of Being as subject (That which is) to Being as attribute (That which It is); and further, since Being-subject is the Knower and Being-attribute (or object) is the Known, this relation is Knowledge itself, but at the same time it is a relation of identity; absolute Knowledge is therefore actual identity, and all true knowledge, being a participation therein, also implies identity insofar as it is effective. It should be added that as the relation draws its reality solely from the two terms it connects, and as these two are in fact only one, it follows that all three elements (Knower, Known, and Knowledge) are truly one only,[2] which can be expressed by saying that 'Being knows Itself by Itself'.[3]

---

2. See what is said about the ternary *Sachchidānanda* in *Man and His Becoming*, chap. 14.

3. In Islamic esoterism, formulas such as the following are also found: 'Allah has created the world from Himself by Himself in Himself,' or again, 'He has sent His message from Himself to Himself by Himself.' These formulas, moreover, are equivalent, for the Divine Message is the 'Book of the World', the archetype of all sacred books, and the 'transcendent letters' that compose that Book are all creatures, as was explained earlier. It follows from this that the 'science of letters' (*'ilm al-ḥurūf*), taken in its highest meaning, is the knowledge of all things in the Principle itself, as

The traditional value of the formula that has just been expressed appears clearly from the fact that it is found in the Hebrew Bible, in the account of God's manifestation to Moses in the Burning Bush.[4] When Moses asks what is His Name, He replies: *Eheieh asher Eheieh*,[5] which is usually translated 'I am Who am' (or 'I am That I am'), but the most exact rendering of which is 'Being is Being.'[6] In fact, Being having been postulated, what can be said of It (and, one must add, what cannot but be said of It) is first that It is, and then that It is Being; these necessary affirmations essentially constitute the whole of ontology in the proper sense of the word.[7] The second way of envisaging the same formula is to postulate first of all the first *Eheieh*, then the second one as the reflection of the first in a mirror (image of the contemplation of Being by Itself); and in the third place the 'copula' *asher* sets itself between those two terms as a link expressing their reciprocal relationship. This corresponds exactly to

eternal essences; in what might be called its middle sense, it is cosmogony; lastly, in its lowest sense, it is the knowledge of the powers of names and numbers, insofar as they express the nature of each being, a knowledge which, by reason of this corre-spondence, permits action of a 'magical' order to be exerted, by their means, upon the beings themselves.

4. Exod. 3:14.

5. In certain schools of Islamic esoterism, the 'Burning Bush', a support of the divine manifestation, is taken as a symbol of the individual appearance persisting after the being has attained to the 'Supreme Identity', in the case parallel to that of the *jīvan-mukta* in the Hindu doctrine (see *Man and His Becoming*, chap. 23); it is the heart resplendent with the light of the *Shekinah*, by the effectively realized presence of the 'Supreme Self' at the center of the human individuality.

6. Here, in fact, *Eheieh* must be regarded as a noun, not a verb and this appears in the context that follows, wherein Moses is enjoined to tell the people: '*Eheieh* hath sent me to you.' As for the relative pronoun *asher*, 'who', when it plays the part of the 'copula', as here, it has the sense of the verb 'to be', for which it does duty in the proposition.

7. The famous 'ontological argument' of Saint Anselm and Descartes, which has given rise to so many discussions, and in fact is highly debatable in the 'dialectical' form in which it has been put forward, becomes perfectly useless, just as any other reasoning does, if, instead of speaking of the 'existence of God' (which indeed implies a mistake as to the meaning of the word 'existence'), one simply puts forward the formula 'Being is', which is self-evident, depending on intellectual intuition and not on the discursive reason (see *Introduction to the Study of the Hindu Doctrines*, pt. 2, chap. 6).

what has been stated above: the point, at first unique, then duplicating itself by a polarization which is also a reflection, and finally the relation of distance (an essentially reciprocal one) establishing itself between the two points by the very fact of their confrontation.[8]

8. It need hardly be pointed out that as the Hebrew *Eheieh* is pure Being, the sense of this name is exactly identical with that of *Ishvara* in the Hindu doctrine, which similarly contains in Itself the ternary *Sachchidānanda*.

18

PASSAGE
FROM RECTILINEAR
TO POLAR COORDINATES:
CONTINUITY BY ROTATION

IT IS NOW NECESSARY to return to the last of the geometrical representations that have been mentioned. The introduction of this is tantamount to substituting polar coordinates for the rectilinear and rectangular coordinates of the previous 'microcosmic' representation. Every variation in the radius of the spiral that we have envisaged corresponds to an equivalent variation on the axis that traverses all the modalities, that is, perpendicular to the direction in which the development of each modality takes place. As for the variations on the axis parallel to this last direction, these are replaced by the different positions occupied by the radius in revolving about the pole (the center of the plane or origin of the coordinates), in other words by the variations in its angle of rotation, measured from a given position taken as origin. This initial position, which will be the normal one at the outset of the spiral (the latter starting from the center tangentially to the radius perpendicular to that position) will be that of the radius which, as already said, contains all the extreme modifications (beginning and end) of all the modalities.

But, of all such modalities, not only do the beginning and the end correspond to each other, but each intermediate modification or element of a modality has likewise its corresponding element in

every other, the corresponding modifications being always represented by points lying on one and the same radius issuing from the
pole. If this radius, whichever it may be, is taken as normal at the
origin of the spiral, we shall always get the same spiral, but the figure
as a whole will have turned through a certain angle. In order to represent the perfect continuity between all the modalities and the correspondence of all their elements, the figure would have to be
imagined as simultaneously occupying all possible positions around
the pole, with all these figures interpenetrating one another, since
each of them, in the sum total of its indefinite development, equally
comprises all the points in the plane. Properly speaking, it is only
one and the same figure in an indefinitude of different positions,
which correspond to the indefinitude of values the angle of rotation
can assume, supposing this angle to vary continuously until the
radius, starting from the given initial position, returns after a complete revolution to superimpose itself upon that first position.

On that supposition, we should get the exact image of a vibratory
movement propagating itself indefinitely, in concentric waves,
around its starting-point, in a horizontal plane such as the free surface of a liquid;[1] and that would be the most exact possible geometrical symbol of the integrality of a state of being. Were it desired to
go further into considerations of a purely mathematical order—
which are not to the point here except insofar as they furnish symbolical representations—it could even be shown that the realization
of that integrality would correspond to the integration of the differ-
ential equation expressing the relationship between the concomi-
tant variations of the radius and of its angle of rotation, both
varying together, and one as a function of the other, continuously,
that is, by infinitesimal quantities. The arbitrary constant that figures in the integral would be determined by the position of the
radius taken as origin, and this same quantity, which is fixed for a
given position of the figure, would be bound to vary continuously
from 0 to 2π for all its positions, so that, if we regard the positions as
able to be simultaneous (this amounts to suppressing the temporal

1. What is here in question is what in physics is called the 'theoretical' free surface, for in practice the free surface of a liquid is not indefinitely extended and
never perfectly realizes the horizontal plane.

condition, which endows the activity of manifestation with the particular qualification constituting movement), the constant must be left indeterminate between those two extreme values.

However, it should be carefully noted that these geometrical representations are always to some extent imperfect, as must indeed be the case with any representation or formal expression. In practice, we are naturally obliged to situate them in a particular space, in a given extension; and space, even when envisaged in the whole extension it is capable of, is no more than a special condition which is contained in one of the degrees of universal Existence, and to which (added to or combined with other conditions of the same order) certain of the multiple domains comprised in that degree of Existence are subjected—each of such domains constituting, in the 'macrocosm', the analogue of what in the 'microcosm' is the corresponding state of the being, situated at that same degree. The representation is necessarily imperfect, simply by being enclosed within narrower limits than that which it represents, and indeed it would otherwise be useless.[2] On the other hand, while always remaining included within the bounds of what is conceivable at present, or even the far more restricted bounds of the imaginable (which proceeds wholly from the sensible), the representation will be proportionately less imperfect the less limited it becomes, which really amounts to saying, the higher the power of the indefinite it introduces.[3] In spatial representations, in particular, this is expressed by adding an extra dimension, as has been shown above; however, this question will be further clarified later.

---

2. Hence the higher can never in any way symbolize the lower, but on the contrary is always symbolized by it. Obviously if the symbol is to fulfill its purpose as a 'support', it must be more accessible, and therefore less complex or extended than what it expresses or represents.

3. In infinitesimal quantities there is always something that corresponds exactly, but in an inverse sense, to these increasing powers of the indefinite, namely, the decreasing orders of the infinitesimal quantities. In both cases, a quantity of a certain order is indefinite, in the increasing or the decreasing sense, not only in respect of ordinary fixed quantities, but also in respect of quantities belonging to all the preceding orders of indefinitude. Thus there is no radical heterogeneity between ordinary quantities (considered as variables) and indefinitely increasing or indefinitely decreasing quantities.

19

REPRESENTATION OF THE CONTINUITY BETWEEN THE DIFFERENT STATES OF THE BEING

IN THIS NEW REPRESENTATION, all that has been considered so far is one horizontal plane, that is, one single state of the being. It is now necessary to depict also the continuity between all the horizontal planes, which represent the indefinite multiplicity of all the states. This continuity is geometrically obtainable in a similar manner: instead of supposing the horizontal plane as fixed in three-dimensional space (a supposition which the fact of movement makes as incapable of material realization as is the tracing of a closed curve), we need only suppose that it changes its position imperceptibly, moving parallel to itself, that is, always remaining perpendicular to the vertical axis, in such a way as to meet this axis at all its points in succession, the passage from one point to another corresponding to the completion of one of the spiral turns that we have considered. The spiral movement will here be deemed isochronous, both in order to simplify the representation as much as possible, and also in order to express the equivalence of the multiple modalities of the being in each of its states, when regarded from the point of view of the Universal.

For further simplicity, we may provisionally consider each of the turns as a circumference, as we did in the case of the fixed horizontal plane. Here again, the circumference will not be closed, for when the radius that describes it comes round again and is superimposed on its original position, it will no longer be in the same horizontal plane (deemed fixed, as being parallel to the direction of one of the planes of coordinates and marking a certain definite situation on the axis perpendicular to that direction); the elementary distance that separates the two extremities of this circumference, or rather of the curve supposed to be a circumference, will then be measured, not now on a radius issuing from the pole, but on a line parallel to the vertical axis.[1] These extreme points do not belong to the same horizontal plane, but to two superimposed horizontal planes; they are situated on either side of the horizontal plane considered in the course of its intermediary travel between these two positions (which corresponds to the development of the state represented by that plane), because they mark the continuity of each state of the being with the ones preceding it and immediately following it in the hierarchical scheme of the total being. If we consider the radii which contain the extremities of the modalities of all the states, their superimposition forms a vertical plane of which they are the horizontal straight lines, and this vertical plane is the locus of all the above-mentioned extreme points, which might be called the limiting-points for the different states, as they previously were, from a different standpoint, for the various modalities of each state. The curve that we provisionally regarded as a circumference is actually one turn, of infinitesimal altitude (the distance between two horizontal planes cut by the vertical axis at two consecutive points), of a helix described on a revolving cylinder whose axis is the vertical axis of our representation. Correspondence between the points on successive turns is here marked by their situation on one and the same generatrix of the cylinder, that is, on one and the same vertical line; the points that correspond to one another, throughout the multiplicity of the states of the being, seem to merge when we consider the totality of the three-dimensional space and view them in orthogonal projection on a base plane of the cylinder, that is, on a given horizontal plane.

To complete this representation it is now enough to envisage, simultaneously, on the one hand this helicoidal movement taking

1. Expressed in different terms, it is in the vertical sense that the curve remains open, not in the horizontal sense as previously.

place on a vertical cylindrical system formed by an indefinite multitude of concentric circular cylinders (the radius varying by only an infinitesimal amount from one to another), and on the other hand the spiral movement we considered earlier in each supposedly fixed horizontal plane. As a result of the combination of these two movements, the base plane of the system will be the horizontal spiral, equivalent to the aggregate of an indefinite multitude of non-closed concentric circumferences; but beyond that, in order to carry still further the analogy between the two- and three-dimensional extensions respectively, and also the better to symbolize the perfect mutual continuity of all the states of the being, we shall have to envisage the spiral, not in one position only, but in all positions it can occupy around its center. We shall thus get an indefinite multitude of vertical systems such as the foregoing, having the same axis, and all interpenetrating one another when regarded as coexisting, because each of them equally comprises the totality of the points in one and the same three-dimensional space, in which they are all situated; here again, this is only the same system considered simultaneously in all the indefinite multitude of positions that it can occupy while accomplishing a complete rotation about the vertical axis.

However, the analogy thus established is still not altogether sufficient; but before proceeding further, it should be pointed out that all that has been said is equally applicable to the 'macrocosmic' representation. In that case, the successive turns of the indefinite spiral traced in a horizontal plane, instead of representing the various modalities of one state of a being, would represent the multiple realms of a degree of universal Existence, while the vertical correspondence would be that of each degree of Existence, in each of the given possibilities it comprises, with all the other degrees. It should be added, to avoid mentioning the point again, that this concordance between the 'macrocosmic' and the 'microcosmic' representations will remain valid for the representations that follow.

20

THE UNIVERSAL
SPHERICAL VORTEX

To return to the complex vertical system considered in the last chapter, it will be seen that the three-dimensional space which is filled by this system is not 'isotropic' about the point that is taken as its center: in other words, owing to the fixing of one particular and so to speak 'privileged' direction which is the axis of the system, namely the vertical, the figure is not homogeneous in all directions from that center. On the other hand, in the horizontal plane, when we were simultaneously considering all positions of the spiral about the center, this plane was envisaged homogeneously and under an 'isotropic' aspect in respect of its center. For this to hold good in three-dimensional space, it must be noted that every straight line passing through the center could be taken as the axis of a system such as the one we have been considering, so that any direction can play the part of the vertical direction; similarly since any plane that passes through the center is perpendicular to one of these straight lines, it follows that, correlatively, any direction can play the part of the horizontal direction, or indeed of the direction parallel to any one of the three planes of coordinates. In fact, any plane that passes through the center can become one of these three planes in an indefinite multitude of systems of tri-rectangular coordinates, for it contains an indefinitude of pairs of orthogonal straight lines intersecting at the center (these lines being all the radii issuing from the pole in the depiction of the spiral); and each of these pairs can form any two of the three axes of one of these systems. Just as every point in the space is a potential center, as was said earlier, so any straight line in that space is a potential axis, and, even when the center has already been fixed, each straight line that passes through it is still potentially any one of the three axes. When the central or principal axis of a system has been chosen, it still remains to fix the other two axes in the plane perpendicular to the first and likewise passing through the center; but it is necessary for not only the center itself but also the three axes to be determined before the cross can be actually traced, that is, before the entire space can be really measured in its three dimensions.

All systems such as our vertical representation can be regarded as coexisting and as having respectively as central axes all the straight lines that pass through the center, for in fact they do coexist in the potential state, and besides, this is no bar to afterwards choosing three particular axes of coordinates to which the whole space will be referred. Here again, all the systems in question are really only different positions of one and the same system as its axis assumes every possible position about the center, and the systems interpenetrate for the same reason as before, namely that each of them comprises all the points in the space. One might say that it is the principial point previously mentioned (independent of any determination, and representing the being in itself) that effectuates or realizes this space, hitherto potential only and conceived as a mere possibility of development, by filling its total volume, indefinite to the third power, by the complete expansion of its virtualities in all directions. Moreover, it is in the plenitude of expansion that perfect homogeneity is obtained, just as, conversely, extreme distinction is realizable only in extreme universality;[1] at the central point of the being, as was said earlier, perfect equilibrium is established between the opposing terms of all contrasts and all antinomies to which outward and particular viewpoints give rise.

When all the systems are considered in this manner as coexisting, the directions of space all play the same part and the radiation from the center outward may be regarded as spherical, or rather spheroidal. The total volume, as has been shown, is a spheroid extending

---

1. We here again allude to the union of the two viewpoints of 'unity in plurality' and of 'plurality in unity', which we mentioned previously in connection with the teachings of Islamic esoterism.

indefinitely in all directions, with a surface that is never closed, any more than the curves previously described. Moreover, the plane spiral, when simultaneously envisaged in all its positions, is nothing but a section of that surface by a plane passing through the center. It has been stated that the realization of a plane in its integrality was expressed by the calculation of a simple integral; here, since a volume and not a surface is in question, the realization of the space in its integrality would be expressed by the calculation of a double integral;[2] the two arbitrary constants that would enter into this calculation could be determined by choosing two axes of coordinates, the third axis being thereby fixed, since it must be perpendicular to the plane of the two others and must pass through the center. It should further be observed that the deployment of this spheroid is ultimately nothing other than the indefinite propagation of a vibratory movement (or 'undulatory', for these two terms are ultimately synonymous), no longer in a horizontal plane only, but in the whole three-dimensional space, of which the starting-point of this movement may now be regarded as the center. If this space is regarded as a geometrical, that is, a spatial symbol of total Possibility (a necessarily imperfect symbol, because limited by its very nature), then the representation at which we have finally arrived will be the depiction—insofar as such a thing is possible—of the universal spherical vortex by which the realization of all things is accomplished, and which the metaphysical tradition of the Far East calls *Tao*, that is, the 'Way'.

2. A point which it is important to bear in mind, though it cannot be dwelt on at present, is that an integral cannot be calculated by taking each of its elements one by one in succession, for in that way, the calculation would never be completed. Integration can be achieved only by a single synthetic operation and the analytical procedure of formation of arithmetical sums cannot be applied to the indefinite. [This subject has been fully dealt with by Guénon in *The Metaphysical Principles of the Infinitesimal Calculus*, chap. 21, 'The Indefinite is Analytically Inexhaustible', and chap. 22, 'Synthetic Character of Integration'. ED.]

21

DETERMINATION OF ELEMENTS IN THE REPRESENTATION OF THE BEING

IN THE PRECEDING CHAPTER, the universalization of our geometrical symbol has been carried to the furthest limits conceivable (or rather, imaginable, since it is always a representation of the sensible order that is involved); and this has been done by gradually introducing into it, in a number of successive phases (or, to speak more exactly, phases successively envisaged in the course of this study), an increasingly greater indetermination, answering to what we have called the increasingly higher powers of the indefinite, but always without departing from three-dimensional space. On arriving at this point, it will be necessary to retrace the same path, as it were, in order to determine positively all the elements in the figure, for without such determination, although the figure exists quite complete in the virtual state, it cannot be actually traced. But this determination, which at the outset was envisaged only hypothetically so to speak, and as a mere possibility, will now become real, for we shall be able to show the exact significance of each of the elements that constitute the cruciform symbol.

What will first be considered is not the universality of beings, but one single being in its totality; the vertical axis will be assumed to be given, and hence the plane passing through that axis and containing the extreme points of the modalities of each state. We shall thus get back to the vertical system whose base is the horizontal spiral considered in one single position. This system has already been described. Here, the directions of the three axes of coordinates are given, but only the vertical one is in fact determined in position; one of the two horizontal axes will lie in the vertical plane just mentioned, and the other will naturally be perpendicular to it; but the horizontal plane that contains these two straight lines still remains undetermined. If we were to determine this plane, we should also thereby determine the center of the space, that is, the origin of the system of coordinates to which that space is referred, since that point is none other than the intersection of the horizontal plane of coordinates with the vertical axis. All elements in the figure would then in fact be determined, and this would allow the tracing of the three-dimensional cross which measures the extension in its totality.

It should again be recalled that, in order to constitute the system representing the total being, we have had to consider first a horizontal spiral and then a vertical cylindrical helix. If we consider in isolation any one turn of such a helix, and if we neglect the elementary difference of level between its two ends, we may regard it as a circle described in a horizontal plane; each turn of the horizontal spiral can similarly be taken as a circumference, if the elementary variation of the radius between its two ends is neglected. Consequently, every circumference described in a horizontal plane and having as its center the actual center of the plane, that is to say its intersection with the vertical axis, can conversely, and with the same approximations, be envisaged as a turn belonging at once to a vertical helix and to a horizontal spiral;[1] it follows that the curve we are representing as a circumference is strictly speaking neither closed nor plane.

Such a circumference will represent any one unspecified modality of an equally unspecified state of the being, envisaged along the vertical axis, which will project itself horizontally in a point (the center of the circumference). If, however, it were envisaged along either of the two horizontal axes, it would project itself in a segment—symmetrical in respect of the vertical axis—of a horizontal straight line which, taken with the latter, forms a two-dimensional cross, this

---

1. This circumference is the same as that which externally bounds the figure known by the name of *yin-yang* in the Far-Eastern symbolism, a figure which will be specially dealt with a little later on.

horizontal straight line being the tracing, on the vertical plane of projection, of the plane in which the circumference in question is situated.

As regards the significance of the circumference and the central point, the latter being the tracing of the vertical axis on a horizontal plane, it should be pointed out that according to a quite general symbolism the center and the circumference represent the starting-point and the termination of any one mode of manifestation.[2] They therefore respectively correspond to what, in the Universal Order, are 'essence' and 'substance' (*Purusha* and *Prakriti* in the Hindu doctrine), or again Being in itself and its possibility, and for any mode of manifestation they depict the more or less particular expression of these two principles regarded as complements, active and passive in their mutual relationship. This finally justifies what was said before about the relation between the different aspects of the symbolism of the cross, for it follows that in our geometrical representation the horizontal plane (which is deemed fixed *qua* plane of coordinates, though it may occupy any position, being determined in direction only) will play a passive part in respect of the vertical axis, which amounts to saying that the corresponding state of the being will be realized in its integral development under the active influence of the principle that is represented by the axis;[3] this will become more intelligible in what follows, but it was important to point it out here and now.

2. It has been seen that in the symbolism of numbers this figure corresponds to the denary, envisaged as the complete development of unity.

3. If we consider the two-dimensional cross obtained by projection upon a vertical plane, a cross naturally formed by one vertical and one horizontal line, we see that under these conditions the cross truly symbolizes the union of the active and passive principles.

22

THE FAR-EASTERN
SYMBOL OF *YIN-YANG*:
METAPHYSICAL
EQUIVALENCE OF
BIRTH AND DEATH

To RETURN TO THE DETERMINATION OF our figure, there are ultimately only two things that call for particular consideration,
namely the vertical axis on the one hand, and the horizontal plane
of coordinates on the other. We know that a horizontal plane represents one state of the being, each modality of which corresponds to
a spiral turn that we have merged into a circumference; however,
the ends of the turn do not actually lie in the plane of the curve, but
in two immediately adjacent planes, for this curve, as conceived in
the vertical cylindrical system, is an element of a helix whose pitch
is infinitesimal. 'On that account, although we at present live, act,
and reason about contingencies, we can and even must regard the
graph of individual evolution[1] as a (plane) surface. Indeed, it possesses all the attributes and qualities of one, and only differs from
a surface when regarded in the Absolute.[2] Thus, on our plane (or

---

1. Either for one particular modality, or even for the integral individuality if it
is considered in isolation in the being; when only one state is considered, the representation must be planar. To forestall any misunderstanding, let it again be recalled
that for us the word 'evolution' can mean nothing more than the development of a
given set of possibilities.
2. That is, when envisaging the being in its totality.

degree of existence), the *circulus vital* is an immediate truth, and the circle is indeed the representation of the human individual cycle.'[3]

The *yin-yang*, which in traditional Far-Eastern symbolism depicts the 'circle of individual destiny', is in fact a circle, for the above reasons. 'It is a circle representative of an individual or specific[4] evolution, and only in two dimensions does it participate in the universal cyclic cylinder. Having no thickness, it has no opacity, and is represented as diaphanous and transparent. In other words the graphs of the evolutions prior and posterior to its moment[5] are seen and imprinted on the sight through it.'[6] But, of course, 'it must never be forgotten that if, taken by itself, the *yin-yang* can be regarded as a circle, in the succession of individual modifications[7] it is an element of a helix: any individual modification is essentially a

3. Matgioi, *La Voie Métaphysique* [Paris: Les Éditions Traditionnelles, 1936], p128.

4. The species, in fact, is not a transcendent principle in respect of the individuals that compose it; it does not surpass, but belongs to, the order of individual existences; accordingly it is situated at the same level of universal Existence, and participation in the species may be said to take place in a horizontal direction. Perhaps it will one day be possible to devote a special study to this question of the conditions of the species.

5. These evolutions are the development of the other states, divided thus in respect of the human state. Metaphysically, it should be recalled, there can never be any question of 'anteriority' or 'posteriority' except in the sense of a causal and purely logical concatenation, which cannot exclude the simultaneousness of all things in the 'eternal present'.

6. Matgioi, op. cit., p129. The figure of the *yin-yang* is divided into two parts, one dark and one light, which respectively correspond to these anterior and posterior evolutions, for in respect of the human state the former states can be symbolically regarded as dark and the latter ones as bright; at the same time the dark part is the side of the *yin* and the light part the side of the *yang*, in conformity with the original significance of these two terms. Again, since *yang* and *yin* are also the masculine and feminine principles, what we get from another point of view, as was indicated earlier, is a representation of the primordial 'Androgyne', the two halves of which are already differentiated but not yet separated. Finally, as representing the cyclic revolutions, whose phases are linked to the alternate predominance of *yang* and *yin*, the same figure is again related to the symbol of the *swastika*, as also to that of the double spiral mentioned earlier. [See *The Great Triad*, chaps. 4–6. ED.]

7. Considered insofar as they correspond to one another (in logical succession) in the different states of the being, which however must be viewed in simultaneity for the different spires of the helix to be mutually comparable.

three-dimensional vortex;[8] there is only one human stage, and the course once completed is never covered again.'[9] The two ends of each turn of a helix of infinitesimal pitch, as was said before, are two immediately adjacent points on a generatrix of the cylinder, which is parallel to the vertical axis (and moreover situated in one of the planes of coordinates). These two points do not really belong to the individuality, or, more generally, to the state of being represented by the horizontal plane under consideration. 'Entry into the *yin-yang* and emergence from the *yin-yang* are not within the individual's power to command, for they are two points which, while belonging to the *yin-yang*, belong also to the spiral inscribed on the lateral [vertical] surface of the cylinder, and which are subject to the attraction of the "Will of Heaven". And indeed, man is not free as to either his birth or his death. As regards his birth, he is free neither to accept nor to refuse nor to choose the moment. As regards his death, he is not free to escape it; and neither can he be free, in all analogical justice, as regards the moment of his death.... In any case, he is not free from any of the conditions of the two acts; birth irresistibly launches him upon the round of an existence that he has neither asked for nor chosen; death withdraws him from that round and irresistibly launches him upon another, prescribed and fore-known by the "Will of Heaven", without his being able to modify it in any respect.[10] Thus, man on earth is a slave as regards his birth and death, that is, in respect of the two chief acts of his individual life, the only ones which finally summarize his special evolution in

8. It is an element in the universal spherical vortex previously described; there is always analogy and a sort of 'proportionality' (without its being possible, however, for there to be any common measure) between the whole and each of its even infinitesimal elements.

9. Matgioi, op. cit., pp131–132 (note). This again formally excludes the possibility of 'reincarnation'. In this respect, it might also be observed, from the viewpoint of the geometrical representation, that a straight line can meet a plane in one point only; this applies, in particular, to the vertical axis in respect of each horizontal plane.

10. This is so because the individual as such is only a contingent being and does not carry within him his own sufficient reason. That is why the course of his existence, if looked at without taking account of the variation in the vertical direction, appears as the 'cycle of necessity'.

regard to the Infinite.'[11] It should be clearly appreciated that 'the phenomena "birth" and "death", regarded in themselves and apart from the cycles which lie between them, are perfectly equal';[12] it can even be said that this is really only one and the same phenomenon envisaged on two opposite sides, from the standpoint of one and the other of the two consecutive cycles between which it is interposed. This indeed emerges at once in our geometrical representation, because the end of any one cycle always and necessarily coincides with the beginning of another, and because we use the words 'birth' and 'death', in their altogether general acceptation, merely to denote the passage from cycle to cycle, and whatever may be the scope of such cycles, which may just as well be those of worlds as of individuals. These two phenomena 'accordingly accompany and complete each other: human birth is the immediate result of a death [to another state]; human death is the immediate cause of a birth [likewise into another state]. Neither of these circumstances can ever occur without the other. And, as time does not exist here, it can be affirmed that, between the intrinsic value of the phenomenon birth and the intrinsic value of the phenomenon death, there is metaphysical identity. As for their relative value, and by reason of the immediacy of the results, death at the end of a given cycle is higher than birth into the same cycle, by the whole value of the attraction of the "Will of Heaven" upon that cycle, that is, mathematically, the pitch of the evolutive screw.'[13]

11. Matgioi, op. cit., pp132–133. 'But, between birth and death, the individual is free, in the putting forth and the directing of all his earthly acts; in the *circulus vital* of the species and the individual, the attraction of the "Will of Heaven" does not make itself felt.'

12. Ibid., pp138–139 (note).

13. Ibid., p137. On this question of the metaphysical equivalence of birth and death, see also *Man and His Becoming*, chaps. 8 and 17.

23

SIGNIFICANCE OF
THE VERTICAL AXIS:
INFLUENCE OF THE
WILL OF HEAVEN

It follows from what has gone before that the pitch of the
helix—the element by which the extremities of any individual cycle
elude the proper domain of the individuality—is the measure of the
'attractive force of the Divinity.'[1] The influence of the 'Will of
Heaven' on the being's development is therefore measured parallel
to the vertical axis; this clearly implies the simultaneous consideration of a plurality of states, forming so many integral cycles of
existence (horizontal spirals) since this transcendent influence does
not make itself felt within a single state taken in isolation.

The vertical axis thus represents the metaphysical locus of the
manifestation of the 'Will of Heaven', and passes through each horizontal plane at its center, that is, at the point where the equilibrium
which that manifestation implies is achieved; in other words, the
point of complete harmonization of all the elements that go to
make up that particular state of the being. This, as was shown earlier, is what must be understood by the 'Invariable Middle' (*Ching-
yung*), and can be considered as a reflection, in each state of the
being (through the equilibrium which is a sort of image of the principial Unity in the manifested order), of the 'Activity of Heaven',
which in itself is non-acting and non-manifested, though it must be
conceived as capable of action and manifestation (yet without being

---

1. Matgioi, *La Voie Métaphysique*, p95.

thereby affected or modified in any way whatever), and indeed as capable of all action and all manifestation, precisely because it is beyond all particular actions and particular manifestations. Consequently, it is possible to say that in the representation of a being, the vertical axis is the symbol of the 'personal Way'[2] which leads to Perfection, and which is a specification of the 'universal Way' represented previously by an indefinite, non-closed spheroidal figure. This specification is obtained, as has been indicated, by the determination of one particular direction in space, namely that of the vertical axis.[3]

Mention has just been made of Perfection, and on this subject a short explanation is necessary. When the term is employed thus, it must be taken in its absolute and total sense. However, in order to be able to think about it in our present condition (as beings pertaining to the individual human state), this concept has to be rendered intelligible in distinctive mode, and this intelligible concept is 'active perfection' (*Ch'ien*), the possibility of the will in Perfection, and naturally of omnipotence, which is identical with what is termed the 'Activity of Heaven'. But, in order to be able to speak about it, the intelligible conception has further to be rendered sensible (because language, like every other outward expression, is necessarily of the sensible order); and it is then 'passive perfection' (*Ch'uan*), the possibility of action as motive and goal. *Ch'ien* is the will capable of manifesting itself, and *Ch'uan* is the object of this manifestation; but, in addition, as soon as one says 'active perfection' or 'passive perfection', one no longer says Perfection in the absolute sense, since there is already a distinction and a determination, and accordingly a limitation. Again, if desired, *Ch'ien* can be called the acting faculty (it would be more correct to say 'influencing'), corresponding to 'Heaven' (*T'ien*), and *Ch'uan* the plastic faculty, corresponding to 'Earth' (*Ti*); here, in Perfection, we find the analogues, though still

2. It should be borne in mind that metaphysically the 'personality' is the transcendent and permanent principle of the being, whereas the 'individuality' is only a transient and contingent manifestation of it.

3. This throws further light on the relationship between the 'Way' (*Tao*) and 'Uprightness' (*Te*).

more universal, of what have been distinguished, in Being, as 'essence' and 'substance'.[4] In any event, whatever the principle by which *Ch'ien* and *Ch'uan* are determined, it must be realized that, metaphysically, they exist only from our viewpoint as manifested beings, just as Being is not polarized and specified into 'essence' and 'substance' in itself, but only in relation to us, and insofar as we envisage it from the standpoint of universal manifestation, of which it is the principle and to which we belong.

Returning to the geometrical representation, we see that the vertical axis is determined as the expression of the 'Will of Heaven' in the being's development, and this fact at the same time determines both the direction of the horizontal planes, representing the different states, and the horizontal and vertical correspondence of these states, thereby establishing their hierarchical arrangement. As a result of this correspondence, the limiting points of these states are determined as extremities of particular modalities; the vertical plane which contains them is one of the planes of coordinates, as is also the one perpendicular to it along the axis. In each horizontal plane these two vertical planes trace a two-dimensional cross, whose center is at the 'Invariable Middle'. Thus there remains only one undetermined element, namely the position of the particular horizontal plane that will be the third plane of coordinates; to this plane there corresponds, in the total being, a certain state, the determination of which will make it possible to trace the symbolic three-dimensional cross, in other words to achieve the actual totalization of the being.

One further point, which it is important to note before going further, is that the vertical distance between the extremities of any evolutive cycle is constant. From this it would seem that whatever the cycle envisaged, the 'attractive force of the Divinity' always acts with the same intensity. This is in fact so in regard to the Infinite, and is expressed by the law of universal harmony, which demands

4. See also *Man and His Becoming*, chap. 4. In the *K'ua* of Fu Hsi, *Ch'ien* is represented by three full strokes and *Ch'uan* by three broken ones; it has already been shown that the full stroke is the symbol of *yang* or the active principle, and the broken stroke that of *yin* or the passive principle.

the quasi-mathematical proportionality of all variations. It is true, however, that to all appearances it might no longer be the same if one adopted a specialized point of view, and had regard only to the course of one given cycle which it was desired to compare with the others in the respect in question. In that case, it would be necessary to find out the value of the pitch of the helix for the exact case in which one had placed oneself (admitting that it would be possible to actually place oneself there, which is in any event outside the viewpoint of pure metaphysics); but 'we do not know the essential value of this geometrical element, because we are at present unaware of the cyclic states through which we have passed, and we cannot therefore measure the metaphysical altitude that today separates us from the one we have emerged from.'[5] We have thus no direct means of appraising the measure of action of the 'Will of Heaven'; 'We should know it only by analogy [by virtue of the law of harmony], if in our present state, being aware of our preceding one, we were able to assess the metaphysical quantity acquired,[6] and hence to measure the upward force. The thing is not said to be impossible, for it is readily comprehensible; but it is not within the faculties of the present humanity.'[7] We would also observe in passing, and simply in order to point out (as we do whenever the opportunity arises) the concordance between all traditions, that what has just been said about the significance of the vertical axis provides a metaphysical interpretation of the well-known Gospel saying to the effect that the Word (or 'Will of Heaven' in action) is (with respect to ourselves)

5. Matgioi, op. cit., pp137–138 (note).

6. Naturally the term 'quantity', here justified by the use of the mathematical symbolism, must be taken in only a quite analogical sense; the same is true of the word 'force' and all others that conjure up images borrowed from the sensible world.

7. Ibid., p96. In this last quotation we have introduced some modifications, but without altering the meaning, so as to apply to each being what was said of the Universe as a whole. 'Man has no power over his own life, because the law that governs life and death, his own mutations, escapes him; what then can he know of the law that governs the great cosmic mutations, the development of the universe?' (*Chuang Tzu*, chap. 25). In the Hindu tradition, the *Purāṇas* state that there is no measure between prior and posterior *Kalpas*, that is, cycles relating to other degrees of universal Existence.

'the Way, the Truth and the Life.'[8] If we go back for a moment to the original 'microcosmic' representation and consider its three axes of coordinates, then the 'Way' (specified in regard to the being envisaged) will be represented, as here, by the vertical axis; of the two horizontal axes, one will then represent the 'Truth' and the other the 'Life'. Whereas the 'Way' is related to 'Universal Man', with whom the 'Self' is identified, the 'Truth' is there related to intellectual man, and the 'Life' to corporeal man (though this last term is also capable of a certain transposition);[9] of the last two, which both belong to one and the same particular state, in other words to one and the same degree of universal Existence, the former must here be assimilated to the integral individuality, of which the latter is only a modality. The 'Life' will then be represented by the axis parallel to the direction in which each modality develops, and the 'Truth' by the axis which connects all the modalities together by running through them at right angles to that direction (this axis, though likewise horizontal, may be regarded as relatively vertical in respect of the other, in accordance with what was said earlier). This, moreover, supposes that the tracing of the three-dimensional cross is related to the earthly human individuality, for it is only in relation to this that we have been considering the 'Life' and even the 'Truth'; this tracing depicts the action of the Word in the realization of the total being and its identification with 'Universal Man'.

8. To forestall any possible misunderstanding, it is as well to specify that what is involved here is exclusively a metaphysical interpretation, and in no wise a religious one; between the two points of view there is all the difference that exists in Islam between the *ḥaqīqah* (the metaphysical and esoteric) and the *sharī'a* (the social and exoteric).

9. These three aspects of man (of which only the last two are 'human' properly speaking) are denoted in the Hebrew tradition by the terms *Adam*, *Aish*, and *Enosh* respectively.

24

THE CELESTIAL RAY
AND ITS PLANE OF
REFLECTION

IF WE CONSIDER the superimposed horizontal planes representing all the states of the being, it can also be said that, whether considered separately or all together, the vertical axis, which connects them all to one another and to the center of the total being, symbolizes what various traditions call the 'Celestial Ray' or 'Divine Ray'. This is the principle which the Hindu doctrine denotes by the names of *Buddhi* and *Mahat*,[1] 'which forms the higher, non-incarnate element in man, and which serves to guide him through the phases of universal evolution.'[2] The universal cycle, represented by our figure as a whole, and

of which humanity [in the individual, specific sense] constitutes only a phase, has a proper movement of its own,[3] independent of our humanity, of all humanities, of all the planes [representing all the degrees of Existence], of which it forms the indefinite sum [which is 'Universal Man'].[4] This proper movement which

---

1. See *Man and His Becoming*, chap. 7, and also chap. 20, for the symbolism of the 'solar ray' (*sushumnā*).
2. Simon and Théophanes, *Les Enseignements secrets de la Gnose*, p10.
3. The word 'movement' again is here a purely analogical expression only, since the universal cycle, in its totality, is obviously independent of the temporal and spatial conditions, as of all other particular conditions whatsoever.
4. This 'indefinite sum' is properly speaking an integral.

it derives from the essential affinity of the 'Celestial Ray' toward its origin, orients it invincibly toward its End [Perfection] which is identical with its Beginning, with an upward and divinely beneficent [that is, harmonic] guiding force,[5]

which is the same thing as that 'force of attraction of the Divinity' referred to in the last chapter.

What must be insisted on is that the 'movement' of the universal cycle is necessarily independent of any individual will whatever, particular or collective, which can operate only within its own particular sphere, and without ever departing from the given conditions of existence to which that sphere is subjected.

Man, *qua* man [individual], cannot dispose of anything more or better than his hominal destiny, the individual course of which he is in fact free to check. But this contingent being, endowed with contingent virtues and possibilities, cannot move, check, or influence himself outside the special contingent plane on which, for the moment, he is placed and exercises his faculties. It is absurd to suppose that he could modify, much less check the eternal course of the universal cycle.[6]

Further, the indefinite extension of the possibilities of the individual, envisaged in his integrality, alters nothing of this, because it naturally cannot release him from the whole set of limiting conditions that characterize the state of being to which he belongs *qua* individual.[7]

The 'Celestial Ray' passes through all the states of the being and, as has already been said, marks the central point of each of them by its trace on the corresponding horizontal plane, and the locus of all these central points is the 'Invariable Middle'; but this action of the 'Celestial Ray' is effective only if by its reflection on one

5. Ibid., p50.
6. Ibid., p50.
7. This is notably true of 'immortality' in the Western sense, that is, conceived as a prolongation of the individual human state in 'perpetuity' or temporal indefinitude (see *Man and His Becoming*, chap. 18).

of those planes it produces a vibration which, by propagating and spreading throughout the whole being, illuminates its cosmic or human chaos. We say cosmic or human, for this can apply to the 'macrocosm' as well as to the 'microcosm'; in all cases, the aggregate of the being's possibilities properly constitutes only a chaos 'without form and void,'[8] wherein there is nothing but obscurity until the moment of this illumination which determines its harmonious organization in the passage from potency to act.[9] This same illumination strictly corresponds to the conversion of the three *gunas* one into another, which was described earlier by reference to a text of the Veda: if the two phases of this conversion are considered, the result of the first, effected as from the lower states of the being, is brought about on the actual plane of reflection, whereas the second phase imparts to the reflected vibration an upward direction, which transmits it throughout the whole hierarchy of the higher states of the being. The plane of reflection, whose center, the point of impact of the 'Celestial Ray', is the starting-point of this indefinite vibration, will then be the central plane in the assemblage of the states of the being, in other words the horizontal plane of coordinates in our geometrical representation, and its center will in fact be the center of the total being. In relation to the 'Celestial Ray' which is the vertical branch of the three-dimensional cross, this central plane, on which its two horizontal branches are traced, plays a part analogous to that of 'passive perfection' in relation to 'active perfection', or that of 'substance' in relation to 'essence', of *Prakriti* in relation to *Purusha*. It is also, symbolically, 'Earth' in relation to 'Heaven', and is identified with what all cosmogonic traditions represent as the 'surface of the Waters'.[10] It can also be described as the plane of separation between the 'Lower Waters' and the 'Upper Waters',[11] that is,

---

8. This is the literal translation of the Hebrew *thohu va-bohu*, which Fabre d'Olivet (*The Hebraic Tongue Restored: And the True Meaning of the Hebrew Words Re-established and Proved by their Radical Analysis*) [New York: G. P. Putnam's Sons, 1921]) explains by 'contingent potency of being in a potency of being.'

9. Cf. Gen. 1:2–3.

10. See *Man and His Becoming*, chap. 5.

11. Cf. Gen. 1:6–7.

the double chaos, formal and formless, individual and extra-individual, of all states, both non-manifested and manifested, the whole array of which constitutes the total Possibility of 'Universal Man'.

By the operation of the 'Universal Spirit' (*Ātmā*), projecting the 'Celestial Ray' which is reflected on the mirror of the 'Waters', there is enclosed within them a divine spark, an uncreated spiritual germ, which, in the potential Universe (*Brahmānda* or 'World Egg'), is the determination of the 'Non-Supreme' *Brahma* (*Aparā-Brahma*) that the Hindu tradition terms *Hiranyagarbha* (that is, the 'Golden Embryo').[12] In each being envisaged in particular, this spark of the intelligible Light constitutes, if one may so put it, a fragmentary unity (an expression that is indeed inaccurate if taken literally, for unity is really indivisible and without parts). This 'fragmentary unity', developing in order to identify itself in act with the total Unity, to which it is identical in potency (for it contains in itself the indivisible essence of light, just as the nature of fire is wholly contained in each spark),[13] will radiate in all directions from the center, and will realize in its expansion the perfect unfolding of all the being's possibilities. This principle of divine essence and indwelling in beings (in appearance only, for it cannot really be affected by contingencies, and this state of 'envelopment' exists only from the viewpoint of manifestation) is again, in the Vedic symbolism, *Agni*[14] manifesting itself at the center of the *swastika*, which as we have seen is the cross traced on the horizontal plane, and which, by its rotation about that center, generates the evolutive cycle that constitutes each of the elements in the universal cycle. The center, the only point that remains motionless in this rotary movement, is by very reason of its immobility (an image of the principial immutability) the mover of the 'wheel of existence'; it contains within it the 'Law' (in the sense

12. See *Man and His Becoming*, chap. 13.
13. See Ibid., chap. 5.
14. *Agni* is depicted as an igneous principle (as indeed is the luminous Ray that gives birth to it), fire being regarded as the active element in relation to water, the passive one. *Agni* at the center of the *swastika* is also the lamb (*agnus*) at the source of the four rivers in the Christian symbolism (see *Man and His Becoming*, chap. 3; *The Esoterism of Dante*, chap. 4; *The King of the World*, chap. 9.

of the Sanskrit term *Dharma*),[15] that is, the expression or manifestation of the 'Will of Heaven' for the cycle corresponding to the horizontal plane in which the rotation takes place, and, following what
was said before, its influence is measured—or rather, would be measured if we had the faculty of doing so—by the pitch of the evolutive
helix on the vertical axis.[16]

The realization of the being's possibilities is thus effected by an
activity which is always inward, since it is exerted from the center of
each plane; moreover, metaphysically, there can be no outward
action exerted upon the total being, for such action is not possible
except from a relative and specialized viewpoint such as that of the
individual.[17] This realization is depicted in different symbolisms by

---

15. See *Introduction to the Study of the Hindu Doctrines*, pt. 3, chap. 5., and *Man
and His Becoming*, chap. 4. For the relationship between the word *Dharma* and the
Sanskrit name for the Pole, *Dhruva*, derived respectively from the roots *dhri* and
dhru, which have the same meaning and essentially express the idea of stability, see
The King of the World, chap. 2.

16. 'When we now [in the course of manifestation] say "The Principle", this
term no longer denotes the solitary Being such as it was primordially; it denotes the
Being that exists in all beings, the universal norm that presides over the cosmic evolution. The nature of the Principle, the nature of Being, are incomprehensible and
ineffable. Only the limited can be understood [in individual human mode] and be
expressed. Of the Principle that acts as the pole, as the axis of the universality of
beings, we only say that it is the pole, that is the axis of universal evolution, without
trying to explain it.' *Chuang Tzu*, chap. 25). That is why the *Tao* 'with a name',
which is 'the Mother of the ten thousand beings' (*Tao Te Ching*, chap. 1) is the
'Great Unity' (*Tai-i*), symbolically located, as was said earlier, in the pole star: 'If it
is necessary to give a name to the *Tao* [although it cannot be named], then it will be
called [as an approximate equivalent] the "Great Unity".... The ten thousand
beings are produced by *Tai-i*, modified by *yin* and *yang*.' In the West, in ancient
'Operative Masonry', a plumb-line, the image of the vertical axis, hangs from a
point that symbolizes the celestial pole. This is also the suspension-point of the
'balance' of which various traditions speak (see *The King of the World*, chap. 10):
and this shows that the 'nothing' (*Ain*) of the Hebrew Kabbalah corresponds to the
'non-acting' (*wu-wei*) of the Far-Eastern tradition.

17. We shall return later to the distinction between the 'inner' and the 'outer',
which is again symbolical, as is all localization; but it should be pointed out that the
impossibility of an outward action applies to the total being only, and not to the
individual being, and that this excludes the parallel one might be tempted to draw
with the assertion, similar in appearance but without any metaphysical bearing,
which the 'monadism' of Leibnitz implies in regard to 'individual substances'.

the opening of a flower on the surface of the 'Waters'. In the Eastern traditions this flower is most commonly the lotus and in the Western ones the rose or lily:[18] but we have no intention of giving a detailed account of these symbols, which may vary and be modified to a certain extent by reason of the manifold adaptations to which they lend themselves, but which always and everywhere ultimately proceed from the same principle, taking into account certain secondary considerations, which are especially based on numbers.[19] In any event, the unfolding in question can first of all be envisaged in the central plane, that is to say in the horizontal plane of reflection of the 'Celestial Ray', as the integration of the corresponding state of the being; but it will also extend outside that plane to the totality of the states, following the indefinite development, in all directions from the central point, of the universal spherical vortex which has already been described.[20]

18. For the relationship between these symbolical flowers and the wheel regarded as a symbol of the manifested world, see *The King of the World*, chap. 2.

19. It has already been stated that the number of spokes in the wheel varies from case to case; the same is true of the petals of the emblematic flowers. The lotus has most frequently eight petals; in Western representations one often finds the numbers 5 and 6, which refer to the 'microcosm' and the 'macrocosm' respectively.

20. On the part played by the 'Divine Ray' in the realization of the being and the passage to the higher states, see also *The Esoterism of Dante*, chap. 8.

25

THE TREE
AND THE SERPENT

IF WE NOW RETURN TO THE SYMBOL of the serpent coiled round a tree, about which a few words were said earlier, it will be observed that this figure is exactly that of the helix traced round the vertical cylinder in the geometrical representation we have been studying. Since the tree symbolizes the 'World Axis', as has been said, the serpent will depict the series of the cycles of universal manifestation;[1] and this accounts for the fact that the traversing of the different states is represented in some traditions as a migration of the being in the body of a serpent.[2] As the traversing can be envisaged in two opposite directions, either upward toward the higher states or downward toward the lower, the two opposed aspects of the serpent symbolism, one benefic and the other malefic, thereby explain themselves.[3]

1. Between this figure and that of the *ouroboros*, that is, the serpent that devours its own tail, there is the same connection as between the complete spiral and the circular figure of the *yin-yang*, in which one of its coils taken separately is regarded as a plane; the *ouroboros* represents the indefinitude of a cycle considered in isolation. Such an indefinitude, for the human state, and owing to the presence of the temporal condition, assumes the aspect of 'perpetuity'.

2. This symbolism is found for example in the Gnostic *Pistis Sophia*, in which the body of the serpent is divided according to the zodiac and its sub-divisions, which moreover brings us back to the figure of the *ouroboros*, for in these conditions all that can be in question is the course of a single cycle, through the diverse modalities of one and the same state; in this case, the migration envisaged for the being is therefore confined to the prolongations of the human individual state.

3. Sometimes the symbol is doubled to correspond to these two aspects, and we get two serpents coiled in opposite directions around a single axis, as in the figure of the caduceus. An equivalent of this is found in certain forms of the Brahmanic staff

The serpent is found coiled not only round a tree, but also round a number of other symbols of the 'World Axis',[4] and especially the mountain, as is seen in the Hindu tradition in the symbolism of the 'churning of the sea'.[5] Here the serpent *Shēsha* or *Ananta*, representing the indefinitude of universal Existence, is coiled round *Meru*, the 'polar mountain',[6] and is pulled in opposite directions by the *Devas* and the *Asuras*, who correspond respectively to the states that are higher and lower than the human; we thus obtain either the benefic or the malefic aspect, according to whether the serpent is regarded from the side of the *Devas* or that of the *Asuras*.[7] Again, if the meaning of the latter is interpreted in terms of 'good' and 'evil', we then get a clear correspondence with the two opposed sides of

(*Brahma-danda*), where we find a double twining of lines which are placed in relation respectively with the two directions of rotation of the *swastika*. This symbolism has manifold further applications, which we cannot possibly go into here; one of the most important is that which relates to the subtle currents in the human being (see *Man and His Becoming*, chap. 20): the analogy of the 'microcosm' and the 'macrocosm' is also valid from this particular point of view.

4. For example, the *omphalos* and certain symbols of the 'World Egg' (see *The King of the World*, chap. 9); in that connection we have called attention to the relation that generally exists between the symbols of the tree, the stone, the egg, and the serpent.

5. This symbolical account is to be found in the *Rāmāyana*.

6. See *The King of the World*, chap. 9.

7. These two aspects can also be related to the two opposed meanings the word *Asura* can itself bear according to the way in which it is dissected: *asu-ra*, 'life-giving'; *a-sura*, 'non-luminous'. Only in the latter sense are the *Asuras* opposed to the *Devas*, whose name expresses the luminosity of the celestial spheres; in the other sense, on the contrary, they are really identified with them (hence the application of the term *Asura*, in certain Vedic texts, to *Mitra* and to *Varuna*). Great care must be taken with this double meaning in order to resolve the apparent contradiction to which it may give rise. If the symbolism of temporal succession is applied to the enchainment of the cycles, one readily appreciates why the *Asuras* are said to be prior to the *Devas*. It is at least curious to note that in the symbolism of the Hebrew Genesis, the creation of the plants before that of the heavenly bodies or 'lights' may be connected with this priority; in fact, according to the Hindu tradition, the plant proceeds from the nature of the *Asuras*, that is, the states lower than the human state, while the heavenly bodies naturally represent the *Devas*, that is, the higher states. In this connection it may be added that the development of 'vegetative essence' in Eden is the development of the germs proceeding from the former cycle, and here the same symbolism also applies.

the 'Tree of Knowledge' and the other similar symbols that have already been examined.[8]

There is yet another aspect of the general symbolism of the serpent in which it appears, not precisely as malefic (which necessarily implies the presence of the benefic correlative, for 'good' and 'evil', like the two terms of any duality, can only be understood by reference to each other), but at any rate as to be dreaded, insofar as it represents the being's attachment to the indefinite series of cycles of manifestation.[9] This aspect belongs for instance to the function of the serpent (or the dragon which is then an equivalent of it) as the guardian of certain symbols of immortality, the approach to which it forbids. Thus we find it coiled round the tree with the golden apples in the garden of the Hesperides, or the beech tree in the wood at Colchis on which the 'golden fleece' hangs; these trees are clearly further forms of the 'Tree of Life' and accordingly they also represent the 'World Axis'.[10]

For the being to realize itself totally, it must escape this cyclic concatenation and pass from the circumference to the center, in other words to the point where the axis meets the plane representing the state in which it is at present situated; the integration of this state

8. In the temporal symbolism, there is also an analogy with the two faces of *Janus*, insofar as one of them is regarded as turned toward the future and the other toward the past. In another study we may one day show, more explicitly than has hitherto been possible, the profound connection between all these symbols from different traditional forms.

9. This is the Buddhist *saṃsāra*, the indefinite rotation of the 'round of existence', from which the being must liberate himself in order to attain *Nirvāṇa*. Attachment to multiplicity is also, in one sense, the Biblical 'temptation', which drives the being away from the original central unity and prevents him from attaining the fruit of the 'Tree of Life'; and this is in fact precisely how the being is subjected to the alternation of the cyclic changes, that is, to birth and death.

10. From a point of view fairly close to the above, we must also mention the symbolic legends which in numerous traditions represent the serpent or dragon as the guardian of 'hidden treasures'; the latter are connected with a number of other very important symbols, such as those of the 'black stone' and the 'subterranean fire' (see *The King of the World*, chaps. 1 and 7); this is again one of the many points that can only be indicated in passing though we may return to it again on another occasion [see also *The Reign of Quantity*, chap. 22. ED.].

having first been thus achieved, the totalization will thereafter take place, starting from that plane as basis, in the direction of the vertical axis. It should be noticed that while there is continuity between all states envisaged in their cyclic course, as was explained before, the passage to the center essentially implies a discontinuity in the being's development; in this respect it may be compared to what from a mathematical standpoint is the 'passage to the limit' of an indefinite series in continuous variation. In fact the limit, being by definition a fixed quantity, cannot as such be attained in the course of the variation, even if this is pursued indefinitely; as the limit is not subject to the variation, it does not belong to the series of which it is the term, and one must go outside that series in order to reach it.[11] Similarly, it is necessary to go outside the indefinite series of manifested states and of their mutations in order to attain the 'Invariable Middle', the fixed and immutable point that commands movement without participating in it, just as the entire mathematical series, in its variation, is ordered by relation to its limit, which thus gives it its law but itself stands outside that law. Metaphysical realization cannot be carried out 'by degrees', any more than can the passage to the limit, or the integration which is really only a sort of particular case of it; it is like a synthesis that cannot be preceded by any analysis, and in face of which all analysis would indeed be powerless and strictly nil in its results.

In the Islamic doctrine there is an interesting and important point in connection with the above. The 'straight path' (*al-ṣirāṭ al-mustaqīm*) which is spoken of in the *Fātihah* (literally 'opening') or first *sūrat* of the Koran, is the same thing as the vertical axis taken in its upward direction, for its 'uprightness' (identical with the *Te* of Lao Tzu) must be envisaged in a vertical direction as is indicated by the root of the word that denotes it (*qām*, 'to raise oneself'). Thus the meaning of the last verse, in which this 'straight path' is defined as the 'path of those on whom Thou pourest forth Thy grace, not that of those on whom Thine anger is, nor of those who are in error.'

11. For a full treatment of this question, see *The Metaphysical Principles of the Infinitesimal Calculus*, chap. 24. ED.

Those on whom the divine 'grace'[12] is, are those who directly receive the influence of the 'Activity of Heaven', and who are led by it to the higher states and to total realization, since their being is in conformity with the universal Will. Again, 'anger' being in direct opposition to 'grace', its action must also be exerted along the vertical axis, but with the opposite effect, which makes it travel downwards, toward the lower states;[13] this is the 'infernal' way opposed to the 'heavenly' way, and these two ways are the lower and upper halves of the vertical axis, starting from the level corresponding to the human state. Lastly, those who are in 'error', in the proper etymological sense of the word, are those who, as is the case with the vast majority of men, drawn and held fast by multiplicity, err or wander indefinitely in the cycles of manifestation, represented by the con-volutions of the serpent coiled around the 'Tree in the Midst'.[14]

In this connection it should again be recalled that the proper meaning of the word *Islam* is 'submission to the divine Will';[15] hence it is said, in certain esoteric teachings, that every being is *muslim*, in the sense that there is clearly none who can elude that Will, and accordingly each necessarily occupies the place allotted to him in the Universe as a whole. The division of beings into 'faithful'

---

12. This 'grace' is the 'falling of dew' which in the Hebrew Kabbalah is placed in direct connection with the 'Tree of Life' (see *The King of the World*, chap. 3).

13. This direct descent of the being down the vertical axis is represented by the 'fall of the angels'; when human beings are involved, this can evidently correspond only to an exceptional case, and such a being is called *Walī ash-shayṭān*, because he is in a way the inverse of the 'saint' or *Walī ar-raḥman*.

14. These three categories of beings might be denoted respectively the 'elect', the 'rejected' and the 'gone astray'; it is worth remarking that they correspond exactly to the three *gunas*; the first to *sattva*, the second to *tamas*, and the third to *rajas*. Some exoteric commentators on the Koran have maintained that the 'rejected' were the Jews and the 'gone astray' were the Christians; but this is a narrow interpretation, highly debatable even from the exoteric point of view, and one that in any case has no sort of explanation according to the *ḥaqīqah*. On the subject of the first of the three categories here in question, it should be pointed out that the 'Chosen One' (*al-Mustafa*) is, in Islam, a title a applied to the Prophet, and, from the esoteric viewpoint, to 'Universal Man'.

15. See *The King of the World*, chap. 6, where the close kinship of this word with those that denote 'health' (or 'salvation') and 'peace' (*as-Salām*) has been indicated.

(*mu'minīn*) and 'infidels' (*kuffār*)[16] thus merely consists in the fact that the former consciously and voluntarily conform to the universal order, whereas among the latter there are some who obey the law only against their will, and others who are in pure and simple ignorance. Here again, then, are the three classes of beings that have just been envisaged; the 'faithful' are those who follow the 'straight path', which is the place of 'peace', and their conformity to the universal Will makes them true collaborators in the 'divine plan'.

16. This distinction does not concern men alone, for the Islamic tradition applies it also to the *Jinn*; in reality, it is applicable to all beings.

26

INCOMMENSURABILITY
BETWEEN THE TOTAL
BEING AND THE
INDIVIDUALITY

IT IS NOW NECESSARY TO DWELL on a point of the first importance. The traditional idea of the being, as set forth in this book, differs essentially and by its very principle from all the anthropomorphic and geocentric ideas which the Western mentality finds
so difficult to surmount. It might even be said to differ infinitely,
and that would be no abuse of language such as occurs on most
occasions when this word is used; on the contrary, it would be a
more accurate expression than any other, and one better suited to
the conception for which we use it, since this is truly unlimited.
Pure metaphysics can in no wise admit anthropomorphism;[1] if the
latter sometimes seems to find its way into metaphysical expression,
that is only a quite outward appearance, and indeed one that is to
some degree inevitable, since any expression necessarily involves the
use of human language. The apparent fault, then, is only a consequence of the imperfection necessarily inherent in all expression,
owing to its very limitation; such a consequence is admitted only by
way of an indulgence, as it were, or a provisional and accidental
concession to the feebleness of the individual human understanding
and its inability to attain to that which transcends the domain of the

1. On this subject, see *Introduction to the Study of the Hindu Doctrines*, pt. 2,
chap. 7.

individuality. Even before any outward expression takes place, this insufficiency already reveals itself in formal thought (which indeed is itself an expression if considered in relation to the formless order): any idea that is thought of with intensity ends by adopting to some extent a human form, namely that of the thinker; to use a striking simile of Shankarāchārya, it might be said that 'thought flows into man as molten metal is poured into the founder's mould.' The very intensity of the thought[2] makes it occupy the whole of the man, more or less as water fills a vessel to the brim; it then assumes the shape of that which contains and limits it, in other words it becomes anthropomorphic. Here again there is an imperfection from which the individual being, under the restricted and particularized conditions of his existence can hardly escape; indeed, in his individual capacity he cannot escape at all, though he is bound to strive toward doing so, for complete release from such limitation is obtained only in the extra-individual and supra-individual—that is, formless—states attained in the course of effective realization of the total being.

Now that this has been said in order to forestall any possible objection on the point, it is clear that there cannot be any common measure between the 'Self', on the one hand, and any individual modification, or even the integrality of a state, on the other. The 'Self', conceived as the totalization of the being, integrates itself by the three dimensions of the cross, and is finally reintegrated into its primal Unity, realized in that very plenitude of expansion of which space in its entirety is but a symbol. An individual human modification is represented by only an infinitesimal element of that space; and even the integrality of a state, depicted by a plane (or at least by something regarded as a plane with the restrictions we have mentioned earlier), still implies only an infinitesimal element of three-dimensional space; the reason is that when this representation is situated in space (that is, amid the array of all the states of the being),

---

2. Of course this word 'intensity' should not be taken in a quantitative sense here. Moreover, since thought is not subject to the spatial condition, its shape is in no way 'localizable'; the order in which it is situated is the subtle, not the corporeal order.

its horizontal plane must be regarded as in fact moving by an infinitesimal quantity along the vertical axis.[3] Since even this necessarily restricted and limited geometrical representation involves infinitesimal elements, it is evident that between what is symbolized by the two terms that have just been compared there is in actual reality and *a fortiori* an absolute incommensurability, not depending on any convention that is more or less arbitrary, as the choice of certain relative units must always be in ordinary quantitative measurements. Again, when the total being is in question, the indefinite is here taken as a symbol of the Infinite, insofar as it is permissible to say that the Infinite can be symbolized; but naturally that in no wise amounts to confusing the two, as is not infrequently done by Western mathematicians and philosophers. 'Although we can take the indefinite as an image of the Infinite, we cannot apply to the Infinite our reasonings about the indefinite; the symbolism descends and does not reascend.'[4]

This integration adds a dimension to the appropriate spatial representation. It is well known in fact that, starting from the line which is the first degree of indefinitude in extension, the single integral corresponds to the calculation of a surface, and the double integral to the calculation of a volume. Therefore, if a first integration has been required in order to pass from the line to the surface, which is measured by the two dimensional cross describing the indefinite circle which never closes (or the horizontal spiral envisaged simultaneously in all possible positions), then a second integration is required in order to pass from the surface to the volume, in which the three-dimensional cross, by the irradiation of its center throughout the directions of the space wherein it is situated, produces the indefinite spheroid, conceived as resulting from a vibratory movement, or in other words the volume, open in all directions, that symbolizes the universal vortex of the 'Way'.

---

3. The question of the fundamental distinction between the 'Self' and the 'ego', that is, ultimately between the total being and the individuality, which was briefly summarized at the beginning of the present study, has been treated more fully in *Man and His Becoming*, chap. 2.

4. Matgioi, *La Voie Métaphysique*, p99.

27

PLACE OF
THE INDIVIDUAL
HUMAN STATE IN
THE BEING AS A WHOLE

FROM WHAT HAS JUST BEEN SAID on the subject of anthropomorphism, it is clear that the human individuality, even when envisaged as an integral whole (and not restricted to the corporeal modality alone), cannot have a privileged and exceptional place in the indefinite hierarchy of states of the total being; it occupies its place among them like any of the other states and by exactly the same right, neither more nor less, in conformity with the law of harmony that governs the relations of all the cycles of universal existence. This place is determined by the particular conditions that characterize the state in question and demarcate its domain. If we cannot at present know what it is, the reason is that we are not able, *qua* human individuals, to get outside these conditions so as to compare them with those of other states, the domains of which are necessarily beyond our reach. But it is obviously sufficient for us, always in our individual capacity, to be aware that this place is what it should be and cannot be other than it is, since each thing is strictly in the situation that it is bound to occupy as an element of the total order. Furthermore, by virtue of the same law of harmony that has just been alluded to, 'the evolutive helix being regular everywhere and at all its points, the passage from one state to another takes place as logically and as simply as the passage from one position (or modification) to another within one and the same state,'[1] without there being, from this point of view at any rate, the least break in continuity anywhere in the Universe.

If we have had to make a reservation as regards continuity (without which universal causality could not be satisfied, demanding as it does that everything should be linked together uninterruptedly) the reason, as was indicated earlier, is that there exists (from a point of view other than that of the course of the cycles) a moment of discontinuity in the development of the being; this moment, which is absolutely unique in character, is that at which the action of the 'Celestial Ray', operating on a plane of reflection, produces the vibration that corresponds to the cosmogonic *Fiat Lux* and illuminates by its irradiation the whole chaos of possibilities. From that moment, chaos is succeeded by order, darkness by light, potency by act, virtuality by reality; and when this vibration has attained its full effect in its amplification and reverberation to the utmost confines of the being, the latter, having thereupon realized its total plenitude, is obviously no longer bound to pass through this or that particular cycle, since it now embraces them all in the perfect simultaneity of a synthetic and 'non-distinctive' comprehension. This is what properly speaking constitutes 'transformation', conceived as implying the 'return of beings in modification into unmodified Being,' outside and beyond all the special conditions that define the degrees of manifested Existence. 'Modification,' says the sage Shi-ping-wen, 'is the mechanism that produces all beings; transformation is the mechanism in which all beings are absorbed.'[2]

This 'transformation' (in the etymological sense of passage beyond form), by which the realization of 'Universal Man' is achieved, is the same thing as 'Deliverance' (in Sanskrit *Moksha* or *Mukti*) of which we have spoken elsewhere;[3] it requires, before all else, the previous determination of a plane of reflection of the 'Celestial Ray', so that the corresponding state thereby becomes the

1. Matgioi, *La Voie Métaphysique*, pp 96–97.
2. Ibid., p 76. For the expression to be correct, it would here be necessary to substitute 'process' for the altogether improper word 'mechanism', borrowed rather unfortunately by Matgioi from Philastre's translation of the *I Ching*.
3. *Man and His Becoming*, chap. 17.

central state of the being. In principle, this can be any state what-ever, since all are quite equivalent when envisaged from the Infinite; and the fact that the human state is in no wise distinguished from the others implies, for it as well as for any other state, the possibility of becoming that central state. 'Transformation' can therefore be attained from the human state as a basis, and even from any modal-ity of that state, which amounts to saying that it is possible for cor-poreal man on earth; in other words, 'Deliverance' can be obtained 'in life' (*jīvan-mukti*),[4] and this does not prevent its essentially implying, for the being who obtains it during human life as in all other cases, absolute and complete release from the limiting condi-tions of all modalities and all states.

As regards the actual process of development which allows the being, after passing through certain preliminary phases, to reach that precise moment when 'transformation' takes place, we have no intention of speaking here, for it is plain that a description of it, even a summary one, cannot enter into the scheme of a work such as this, whose character must remain purely theoretical. All we have sought to do is to show what the possibilities of the human being are; and these possibilities are necessarily possessed by the being in each of its states, for the states cannot differ in any way from one another in respect of the Infinite, in which Perfection resides.

4. Ibid., chap. 18.

28

THE GREAT TRIAD

IF THESE LATEST CONSIDERATIONS are set beside what was said at the beginning, it will readily be appreciated that the traditional idea of 'Universal Man', despite the name, has absolutely nothing anthropomorphic about it. However, while all anthropomorphism is strictly anti-metaphysical and must be rejected as such, it remains to be shown in what sense and under what conditions a certain anthropocentrism may nevertheless be regarded as legitimate.[1]

In the first place, from the cosmic viewpoint mankind performs a 'central' function in respect of the degree of Existence that it belongs to, but in respect of that degree alone, and not, of course, in respect of universal Existence, in which that degree is merely one among an indefinite multitude, with nothing entitling it to a special position as compared with the others. In this regard, then, there can be no question of anthropomorphism except in a restricted and relative sense, yet one sufficient to justify the analogical transposition of the idea of man which gives rise to the term 'Universal Man'.

From another viewpoint, it has been shown already that every human individual (or for that matter any manifestation of a being in any state) contains the possibility of making himself the center in respect of the total being. Thus it can be said that he is the center

---

1. It must be added that this anthropocentrism has no necessary solidarity with geocentrism, despite the affinity which is found between them in certain 'profane' conceptions. What might cause misunderstanding in this respect is that the earth is sometimes taken to symbolize the corporeal state in its entirety; but it is hardly necessary to say that earthly humanity is not the whole of humanity.

virtually, so to speak, and that the goal he must set before himself is to turn that virtuality into a reality. Accordingly, even before such realization, and with a view to it, the being is entitled to place himself as it were ideally at the center.[2] Since he is in the human state, his special perspective naturally endows that state with a preponderant importance which it cannot have from the standpoint of pure metaphysics; and this preponderance will be justified *a posteriori* so to speak in the case when the being, after taking the state in question as its starting-point and basis for realization, succeeds in really making it the central state of its totality, corresponding to the horizontal plane of coordinates in our geometrical representation. This implies, in the first place, that the being in question has been reintegrated into the center of the human state itself (it is in this reintegration that the restitution of the 'primordial state' consists), and thereafter that the center of the human state itself has become identified, for this being, with the universal center. In the first phase the integral human state is realized, in the second the totality of the being.

According to the Far-Eastern tradition, the 'true man' (*cheng jen*) is he who, having realized the return to the 'primordial state', is thenceforth established for good in the 'Invariable Middle', and thereby escapes from the vicissitudes of the 'round of existence'. Above this degree is that of 'transcendent man' (*shen jen*), who strictly speaking is no longer a man, because he has risen above humanity and is wholly emancipated from its specific conditions; he is one who has achieved total realization and attained the 'Supreme Identity', and such a one has therefore truly become 'Universal Man'. This cannot be said of 'true man', yet he can be described as at least virtually 'Universal Man', in the sense that as he has no further states to go through in distinctive mode, because he has passed from the circumference to the center, the human state

---

2. This is somewhat comparable with the way in which Dante, by a temporal and also non-spatial symbolism, places himself at the middle of the 'great year' to accomplish his journey through the 'three worlds' (see *The Esoterism of Dante*, chap. 8).

will necessarily become, for him, the central state of the total being, even though it is not yet so effectively.[3]

It now becomes clear in what sense the middle term of the 'Great Triad' envisaged by the Far-Eastern tradition should be taken; the three terms are 'Heaven' (*T'ien*), 'Earth' (*Ti*), and 'Man' (*jen*), with the third playing the part of 'mediator' between the other two, uniting their two natures in himself. One may truly say, even of individual man, that he participates in 'Heaven' and 'Earth', which are identified with *Purusha* and *Prakriti*, the two poles of universal manifestation; but there is nothing here that is peculiar to the case of man, and one may say the same of any manifested being. In order that man may be effectively able to play the part in question in respect of universal Existence, he must have reached the point of situating himself at the center of all things, in other words he must have attained at least the state of 'true man'; even then, he will actually perform that function for one degree of Existence alone, and only in the state of 'transcendent man' is this possibility realized in its plenitude. This is tantamount to saying that the true 'mediator', in whom the union of 'Heaven' and 'Earth' is fully accomplished by the synthesis of all the states, is 'Universal Man', who is identical with the Word; and, be it noted in passing, many aspects of the Western tradition, even from a purely theological point of view, find here their deeper meaning.[4]

3. The difference between these two degrees is the same as that between what has elsewhere been called virtual immortality and actually realized immortality (*Man and His Becoming*, chap. 18): these are the two stages that we have distinguished from the outset in the realization of the 'Supreme Identity'. In Arabic terminology, the equivalent of 'true man' is 'Primordial Man' (*al-Insān al-qadīm*), and that of 'transcendent man' is 'Universal Man' (*al-Insān al-kāmil*). For the relationship between 'true man' and 'transcendent man' see *The Great Triad*, chap. 18.

4. The union of 'Heaven' and 'Earth' is the same thing as the union of the two natures, divine and human, in the person of Christ, insofar as he is regarded as 'Universal Man'. One of the ancient symbols of Christ is the six-pointed star, that is, the double triangle of the Seal of Solomon (cf. *The King of the World*, chap. 4). In the symbolism of a Hermetic school to which Saint Albert the Great and Saint Thomas Aquinas were attached, the upright triangle represents the Divinity, and the inverted one human nature ('made in the image of God', as His inverted reflection

Again, as 'Heaven' and 'Earth' are two complementary principles, one active and the other passive, their union can be represented by the figure of the 'Androgyne', and this takes us back to what was said earlier in regard to 'Universal Man'. Here again, every manifested being participates in the two principles and this is expressed by the presence of the two terms *yang* and *yin*, but in different proportions and always with one or the other predominating; the perfectly balanced union of the two terms can be realized only in the 'primordial state'.[5] As for the total being, there can no longer be any question of a distinction between *yang* and *yin*, which have then re-entered the principial indifferentiation; accordingly, one can no longer even speak of the 'Androgyne', which already implies a certain duality in unity itself, but only of a 'neutrality' which is that of Being regarded

---

in the 'mirror of the Waters'), so that the combination of the two triangles represents that of the two natures (al-*Lāhūt* and al-*nāsūt* in Islamic esoterism). It should be observed, from the special viewpoint of Hermeticism, that the human ternary *spiritus, anima, corpus* corresponds to the ternary of the alchemical principles 'sulphur, mercury, salt'. Again, from the standpoint of numerical symbolism, the Seal of Solomon is the figure of the number 6, which is the 'conjunctive' number (the letter *vau* in Hebrew and Arabic), the number of union and mediation; it is also the number of creation and, as such, it also befits the Word *per quem omnia facta sunt*. The five- and six-pointed stars respectively represent the 'microcosm' and the 'macrocosm', and also individual man (bound to the five conditions of his state, to which the five senses and the five corporeal elements correspond), and 'Universal Man' or the *Logos*. The function of the Word, in respect of universal Existence, can also be specified by the addition of the cross traced within the figure of the Seal of Solomon; the vertical branch joins the apexes of the two opposed triangles, or the two poles of manifestation, and the horizontal branch represents the 'surface of the Waters'. In the Far-Eastern tradition, we meet with a symbol which, while differing from the Seal of Solomon in arrangement is numerically equivalent to it: six parallel strokes, complete or broken as the case may be (the sixty-four 'hexagrams' of Wen-Wang in the *I Ching*, each of them being formed by the superimposition of two of the eight *K'ua* or trigrams of *Fu Hsi*) constitute the 'graphs of the Word' (in relationship with the symbolism of the Dragon): and they also represent 'Man' as middle term of the Great Triad (the upper 'trigram', corresponding to 'Heaven' and the 'lower one' to 'Earth', and this identifies them respectively with the upright and inverted triangles in the Seal of Solomon).

5. For this reason the two halves of the *yin-yang*, by their union, constitute the complete circular form (which corresponds in the plane to the spherical form in three-dimensional space).

in itself, beyond the distinction between 'essence' and 'substance', 'Heaven' and 'Earth', *Purusha* and *Prakriti*. Only in respect of mani-festation, therefore, can the couple *Purusha-Prakriti* be identified, as was said earlier, with 'Universal Man';[6] and this is clearly the point of view from which the latter is the mediator between 'Heaven' and 'Earth', for these two terms themselves disappear as soon as one passes beyond manifestation.[7]

6. What is here said about the true place of the Androgyne in the realization of the being, and of its relations with the 'primordial state', explains the important part played by this idea in Hermeticism, whose teachings relate to the cosmological domain, as well as to the extensions of the human state in the subtle order, that is in short to what may be called the 'intermediary world', which must not be confused with the domain of pure metaphysics.

7. From this it is possible to understand the higher sense of the Gospel saying: 'Heaven and Earth shall pass away, but my words shall not pass away.' The Word in itself and hence 'Universal Man', which is identical with it, is beyond the distinction between 'Heaven' and 'Earth'. It remains eternally such as it is, in the plenitude of Its Being, when all manifestation and all differentiation (that is, the whole order of contingent existences) have vanished in total 'transformation'.

29

CENTER AND CIRCUMFERENCE

THE FOREGOING BY NO MEANS implies that space can be regarded as 'a sphere which has its center everywhere and its circumference nowhere,' to use the oft-quoted formula of Pascal, who indeed may not have been the first to use it. In any event, there is no need to discuss here what meaning Pascal himself attached to the phrase, which may have been wrongly interpreted, for it is clear that the author of the all-too-famous observations about the 'two infinites', despite his undeniable merits in other respects, did not possess any knowledge of a metaphysical order.[1]

In the spatial representation of the total being, it is undoubtedly true that before any determination has been made, each point is potentially the center of the being who is represented by the extension in which that point is situated; but it is only potentially and virtually so, until the real center has been actually determined. This determination implies that the center is to be identified with the very nature of the principial point, which, in itself, is not properly speaking anywhere, since it is not subject to the spatial condition, and this allows it to contain all the possibilities of that condition. What are everywhere, then, in the spatial sense, are only the principial point's manifestations, which in fact fill space in its entirety,

---

1. A plurality of infinites is obviously impossible, for they would limit one another, so that none of them would really be infinite. Pascal, like many others, confuses the infinite with the indefinite, the latter being understood quantitatively and taken in the two opposing senses of increasing and decreasing magnitudes. [For further remarks on this point, see *The Metaphysical Principles of the Infinitesimal Calculus*. ED.]

but are no more than mere modalities, so that 'ubiquity' is really no more than a sensible substitute for true 'omnipresence'.[2] Furthermore, if the center of space endows as it were with its own nature all other points by the vibration it imparts to them, this is true only insofar as it makes them participate in the same indivisibility and freedom from conditions that it enjoys itself, and this participation, to the extent that it is effective, thereby frees these points from the spatial condition.

It is always desirable to bear in mind the general elementary law that between the fact or sensible object (ultimately the same thing) which is taken as a symbol, and the idea or rather metaphysical principle which it is desired to symbolize as far as that is possible, the analogy is inverse, which is moreover always the case of true analogy.[3] Thus, in space considered in its existing reality, and not as a symbol of the total being, no point is or can be the center; all points equally belong to the domain of manifestation, by the very fact of belonging to space. Space is one of the possibilities whose realization falls within that domain, which, in its entirety, constitutes no more than the circumference of the 'wheel of things', or what might be called the outwardness of universal Existence. Again, of course, to speak here of 'inward' and 'outward', of center and circumference, is to use symbolical language, the language of spatial symbolism; but the impossibility of doing without such symbols proves no more than the inevitable imperfection of our means of expression. If it is possible, up to a certain point, to communicate our ideas to others, in the manifested and formal world, it can obviously only be done through representations that manifest these ideas in certain forms, that is, by correspondence and analogies. This is the principle and final cause of all symbolism; and every expression, whatever its mode, is in reality nothing but a symbol.[4] Only 'let us beware of confusing the thing (or idea) with the deteriorated form under which alone we can depict it, and perhaps even

2. See *Man and His Becoming*, chap. 25.
3. In this connection, compare what was said at the outset about the analogy between individual man and 'Universal Man'.
4. See *Introduction to the Study of the Hindu Doctrines*, pt. 2, chap. 7.

understand it (*qua* human individuals); for the worst metaphysical (or rather, anti-metaphysical) errors have arisen from inadequate comprehension and wrong interpretation of symbols. And let us always remember the god Janus who is depicted with two faces, yet has only one, which is not either of those that we can touch or see.'[5] This image of Janus might be applied with exactitude to the distinction between 'inward' and 'outward', as well as to the consideration of the past and the future; and the single countenance, which no relative and contingent being can behold without first emerging from its limited condition, can correspond exactly to the third eye of *Shiva*, which sees all things in the 'eternal present'.[6]

Under these conditions, if our expression is to conform to the normal relationship of all analogies (which might well be described, in geometrical language, as a relationship of inverse homothesis), the formula of Pascal quoted above should, and indeed must, be reversed. It will then correspond to the Taoist text already quoted:

The point which is the pivot of the norm is the motionless center of a circumference on the rim of which all contingencies, distinctions, and individualities revolve.[7]

At first sight, it might almost be thought that the two images are comparable, but in reality they are the exact reverse of each other. Evidently Pascal let himself be carried away by his geometrician's imagination, which led him to reverse the true relationships as they should be envisaged from a metaphysical standpoint. It is the center that is properly speaking nowhere, because, as has been said, it is essentially 'non-localized': it is not to be found anywhere in manifestation, since it is absolutely transcendent in respect thereof, while being at the center of all things. It is beyond all that lies within the scope of the senses or any faculty proceeding from the sensible order:

5. Matgioi, *Le Voie Métaphysique*, pp 21–22.
6. See *Man and His Becoming*, chap. 20, *The King of the World*, chap. 5, and *The Reign of Quantity*, chap. 23.
7. *Chuang Tzu*, chap. 2.

The Principle cannot be attained by the eye nor the ear.... The Principle cannot be heard; what is heard is not It. The Principle cannot be seen; what is seen is not It. The Principle cannot be stated; what is stated is not It. ...The Principle, being unimaginable, cannot be described either.[8]

All that can be seen, heard, imagined, stated, or described, necessarily belongs to manifestation, and even to formal manifestation; it is therefore really the circumference that is everywhere, since all places in space, or more generally, all manifested things (space being here only a symbol of universal manifestation), 'all contingencies, distinctions, and individualities', are only elements in the 'current of forms', points on the circumference of the 'cosmic wheel'.

Accordingly, to sum up in a few words, it can be said that, not only in space, but in all that is manifested, what is everywhere is the exterior or the circumference, whereas the center is nowhere; since it is unmanifested; but (and here the expression 'inverse sense' takes on the full force of its meaning) the manifested would be absolutely nothing without that essential point, which in itself is not manifested at all, and which, precisely by reason of its non-manifestation, contains in principle all possible manifestations, being the 'unmoved mover' of all things, the immutable origin of all differentiation and modification. This point produces the whole of space (as well as all other manifestations) by as it were issuing from itself and by unfolding its virtualities in an indefinite multitude of modalities, with which it fills space in its entirety; but when we say that it issues from itself to effect this development, such a very imperfect expression must not be taken literally. In reality, since the principial point is never subject to space, which it brings into existence, and since the relationship of dependence (or causal relationship) is obviously not reversible, this point remains 'unaffected' by the conditions of any of its modalities and consequently never ceases to be identical with itself. When it has realized its total possibility, it is only to come back (though the idea of 'returning' or 'beginning again' is in no way applicable here) to the 'end which is identical with the beginning',

8. Ibid., chap. 22. Cf. *Man and His Becoming*, chap. 15.

that is, to the primal Unity which contains everything in principle, a Unity which, being Itself (considered as the 'Self'), can in no wise become other than Itself (for that would imply a duality), and from which, therefore, when considered in Itself, It had never departed. Further, so long as one is dealing with the being as such, and even with universal Being, all one can speak of is Unity, as we have been doing; but if it were sought to transcend the bounds of Being itself and to envisage absolute Perfection, then it would be necessary at the same time to pass beyond that Unity to metaphysical Zero, which cannot be represented by any symbolism, or named by any name.[9]

9. See *Man and His Becoming*, chap. 15.

30

FINAL REMARKS
ON SPATIAL SYMBOLISM

SO FAR, NO ATTEMPT HAS BEEN MADE to draw a distinction between what is meant by 'space' and 'extension', respectively, and in many cases they have been used more or less as synonyms. The distinction between them, like that between 'time' and 'duration', may lend itself to philosophical subtleties, and may even have some real value from a cosmological point of view, but pure metaphysics is not really concerned with it.[1] Besides, in a general way, it is better to keep clear of any complications of language that are not strictly needed for clearness and accuracy of exposition. To use words which are not ours but which we can fully endorse, 'we are reluctant to burden metaphysics with a fresh terminology, remembering that terminologies are subjects of discussion, error, and discredit; those who create them, for the apparent needs of their demonstrations, incomprehensibly damage their texts by them, and become so wedded to them that often these dry, useless terminologies end up by constituting the sole novelty of the proposed system.'[2]

---

1. While extension is usually regarded as a particularization of space, the relationship between time and duration is sometimes envisaged in the opposite sense; according to some conceptions, in fact, and notably those of the Scholastic philosophers, time is only a particular mode of duration; but this, though perfectly acceptable, has little bearing on the present subject. All that need be said is that the term 'duration' is taken to denote any mode of succession in general, that is to say any condition which, in other states of existence, may analogically correspond to what time is in the human state; but the use of the term is perhaps liable to give rise to confusion.

2. Matgioi, *La Voie Métaphysique*, p33 (note).

Apart from these general reasons, if we have in fact often described as space that which is properly speaking only a particular three-dimensional extension, the reason is that, even at the highest degree of universalization of the spatial symbol that has been examined, we have not gone beyond the limits of that extension, which has been taken as giving a representation—necessarily imperfect—of the total being. Nevertheless, if one wished to keep to stricter phraseology, undoubtedly the word 'space' should be used only to denote the sum total of all particular extensions. Thus, the spatial possibility, the 'actualization' of which forms one of the special conditions of certain modalities of manifestation (such as our own corporeal modality, in particular) in the degree of existence that the human state belongs to, contains in its indefinitude all possible extensions, each of which is itself indefinite in a lesser degree, and which can differ from one another by their number of dimensions or by other features; again, clearly, the space known as 'Euclidian', which is studied in ordinary geometry, is only a particular case of a three dimensional extension, since it is not the only conceivable modality of it.[3]

Despite this, the spatial possibility, even in all its generality, is still only one given possibility, indefinite no doubt, even indefinite to a multiple power, but nonetheless finite, because—as is shown in particular by the production of the series of numbers starting from unity—the indefinite proceeds from the finite, which means that the finite itself must potentially contain the indefinite. It is quite obvious that the greater cannot come out of the lesser, nor the infinite out of the finite. Besides, were this not so, the coexistence of an indefinitude of other possibilities, which are not included in the spatial possibility,[4] and each of which is equally capable of an indefinite development, would be impossible. This consideration alone, even failing any other, would fully suffice to prove the absurdity of

---

3. The perfect logical consistency of the various 'non-Euclidian' geometries is proof enough of this; but naturally this is not the place to stress the meaning and scope of these geometries, any more than those of 'hyper-geometry' or the geometry of more than three dimensions. [For this last point, see *The Reign of Quantity*, chaps. 18 and 23. ED.]

4. To keep to what is well known to all, ordinary thought itself, as envisaged by psychologists, is outside space and cannot in any way be situated in it.

the 'infinite space' about which one has heard so much,[5] for nothing can be truly infinite except that which comprehends all, and outside of which there is absolutely nothing that can limit it in any way whatsoever; in other words, total and universal Possibility.[6]

This brings us to the end of the present study, and we must hold over for another occasion an examination of the metaphysical theory of the multiple states of the being considered independently of the geometrical symbolism arising from it.[7] We need only add the following, by way of conclusion. Through consciousness of the permanent Identity of Being throughout all the indefinitely multiple modifications of Existence, there is manifested, at the very center of our human state, as well as at the center of all other states, the transcendent and formless, and hence unincarnated and unindividualized element which is called the 'Heavenly Ray'. This consciousness is therefore higher than any formal faculty, which means that it is essentially supra-rational, and implies intuitive perception of the law of harmony which binds together and unites all things in the Universe; and for our individual being, but independently of it and of the conditions to which it is subject, this consciousness is no less than the 'sense of eternity'.[8]

5. And equally, for that matter, of the 'infinite number'. In general, the alleged 'quantitative infinite', in all its forms, is not and cannot be anything but purely and simply the indefinite. With that, all the contradictions inherent in this so-called infinite, which so greatly embarrass mathematicians and philosophers, disappear.

6. While it is impossible, as was said earlier, to admit the narrow viewpoint of geocentrism, habitually bound up as it is with anthropomorphism, one cannot on that account think any the more highly of the sort of scientific or pseudo-scientific lyricism that seems so dear to the hearts of certain astronomers, and that is forever speaking of 'infinite space' and 'eternal time'. These expressions, let it be said again, are sheer absurdities, for the simple reason that nothing can be infinite but that which is independent of space and time. Ultimately what all this amounts to is another of the numerous attempts by the modern mind to restrict universal Possibility to the measure of its own capacities, which barely go beyond the bounds of the perceptible world.

7. See *The Multiple States of the Being*. ED.

8. Needless to say, the word 'sense' is not here taken in its proper meaning, but must be understood, by analogical transposition, to denote an intuitive faculty which grasps its object immediately, as sensation does in its order; but here there is all the difference that separates intellectual intuition from sense-intuition, the supra-rational from the infra-rational.

INDEX

Greek(s) 12 n2, 24, 63 n2, 90
guna(s) 29–33, 118, 126 n14

Hamsa 18 n4, 37 n7
ḥaqīqah 115 n8, 126 n14
Hebrew 25, 28 n32, 37 n7, 43, 64
    n6, 93–94, 115 n9, 118 n8, 137
Hermetic(ism) 12, 38 n9, 47 n
    32, 59 n24, 136–138
Hermes 57 n15
Hesperides, Garden of 60 n28,
    124
Hindu:
    doctrine 17, 25–26, 43–45, 49–
    50, 52 n7, 61 n32, 70 n1, 89 n6,
    94 n8, 106, 116
    symbolism 25 n18
    terminology 76
    theory 30
    tradition 18 n4, 24 n14, 37 n7,
    44 n18, 52 n6, 56 n9, 59 n24,
    78, 114 n7, 123
Hiranyagarbha 119

I Ching 38 n9, 45 n21, 132 n2,
    137 n4
'ilm al-hurūf 92 n3
India 61–62
Ishvara 26 n22, 94 n8
Islam 17 n2, 115 n8, 126 n14
Islamic:
    esoterism 12, 16–17, 26 n21, 36
    n6, 41, 43–44, 46 n27, 52 n7, 54
    n1, 92–93, 102 n1, 137 n4
    doctrine 49, 125
    initiation 37 n6
    tradition 14 n8, 18 n4, 127 n
    16

Janus 124 n8, 141

jen 135–136
Jerusalem 27 n29, 38 n9, 60
jihād 49–50
jīvan-mukta 45 n23, 93 n5
jīvan-mukti 133
jivātmā 49 n2
Josephus 24
Judeo-Christian tradition 14–15,
    46 n29

Kabbalah 12 n1, 23–25, 43 n16,
    46, 55, 59 ns23 and 24, 120 n16,
    126 n12
Kether 27
Koran 78 n10, 126 n14

Lao Tzu 42, 48 n35, 125
Latvia 62 n2
Leibnitz 7, 18–19, 36 n5, 38 n9, 84
    n6, 88 n4, 120 n17
Lithuania(n) 62 n2

Manicheans 39 n2
Manvantara(s) 24, 61 n32
Meru 59 n24, 123
Moksha (Mukti) 17, 132
Moses 93
Moses de Léon 26
Muḥyi 'Dīn ibn al-'Arabī 12 n1,
    44 n17, 54 n1, 78
Müller, Max 21 n2
Muslim(s) 17 n2, 126

Nietzsche 83 n5
Nirvāna 41 n5, 124 n9

ouroboros 122 ns1 and 2

Pascal 139, 141
Persian(s) 17 n2, 24

Ingram Content Group UK Ltd.
Milton Keynes UK
UKHW031305050523
421296UK00001B/17